Radical Freedom

Breaking the Chains of Addiction for Good

MELISSA HURAY

BroadStreet
PUBLISHING

BroadStreet Publishing® Group, LLC
Savage, Minnesota, USA
BroadStreetPublishing.com

Radical Freedom: Breaking the Chains of Addiction for Good
Copyright © 2024 Melissa Huray

9781424567126 (faux leather)
9781424567133 (ebook)

Scripture quotations marked NKJV are taken from the New King James Version®. Copyright © 1982 by Thomas Nelson. Used by permission. All rights reserved. Scripture quotations marked NLT are taken from the Holy Bible, New Living Translation. Copyright © 1996, 2004, 2015 by Tyndale House Foundation. Used by permission of Tyndale House Publishers, a Division of Tyndale House Ministries, Carol Stream, Illinois 60188. All rights reserved. Scripture quotations marked NIV are taken from The Holy Bible, New International Version® NIV®. Copyright © 1973, 1978, 1984, 2011 by Biblica, Inc.™ Used by permission. All rights reserved worldwide. Scripture quotations marked ESV are taken from the ESV® Bible (The Holy Bible, English Standard Version®). Copyright © 2001 by Crossway, a publishing ministry of Good News Publishers. Used by permission. All rights reserved. Scripture quotations marked NASB are taken from the New American Standard Bible® (NASB). Copyright © 1960, 1962, 1963, 1968, 1971, 1972, 1973, 1975, 1977, 1995, 2020 by The Lockman Foundation. Scripture marked KJV are taken from the King James Version of the Bible, public domain. Scripture quotations marked ASV are taken from the American Standard Version, public domain. Scripture quotations marked NLV are taken from the *New Life Version*. Copyright © 1969 and 2003. Used by permission of Barbour Publishing, Inc., Uhrichsville, Ohio 44683.

Cover and interior by Garborg Design Works | garborgdesign.com

Printed in China

24 25 26 27 28 5 4 3 2 1

The bondage to addiction brings a great deal of regret, pain, and brokenness. It's time to stop feeling ashamed of your story and instead let God use it to lead others out of the darkness. It is through this lens that I wrote this devotional for you.

Introduction

I spent fifteen years on the merry-go-round of binge drinking, routinely to the point of blacking out. I experienced a great deal of shame and embarrassment because of it, and it sent me on a desperate, endless search for answers.

I visited self-help groups, saw therapists, read books, and followed gurus. I exhausted myself trying to follow a million broken pieces of well-intentioned advice. Everything offered a small amount of relief, but nothing lasted. Most literature I investigated suggested that the only remedy was white-knuckling through life and hoping to avoid relapse. The idea that I was saddled with a "disease" forever made me feel completely hopeless that I would ever truly change. I wanted total freedom. I finally found it, but not through the world's offerings.

Addictive choices are sinful and idolatrous and require repentance and the power of the Holy Spirit to change. A Christ-centered approach to addiction recovery illuminates the message of hope found in the Bible. God has taken a tapestry of life experience—addiction, binge eating, divorce, spiritual warfare, forays into the occult, and marital brokenness—and turned it all for the good. These experiences became the content for this book.

I believe the Holy Spirit inspired the words on these pages and delivered them through me. I hope you find healing in this devotional, and I hope it helps lead you to a relationship with Jesus Christ, who yearns to show you the way out. He is the doorway to total freedom.

January

All Things New

"I am doing a new thing;
now it springs forth, do you not perceive it?
I will make a way in the wilderness and rivers in the desert."

ISAIAH 43:19 ESV

There is nothing quite like the fresh start that comes with turning the calendar to a brand-new year. But for someone struggling with addiction, each morning is simply a repeat of the one before—shame, dread, withdrawal, and lies. Fudging the truth, cheating, and hiding are their tired, old companions greeting them each new day. The voice of the Enemy and self-delusion deceive them into believing things will be different, but things will never change as long as they refuse to accept the truth. It's time to face reality: our behaviors, compulsions, and refusal to repent are slowly killing us. Jesus offers us an abundant life, but it will remain out of reach until we surrender and repent. Today is the day to renounce the idolatry of addiction and to take the first step toward freedom.

Surrender

Today I decide to stop addictive behaviors. I will list new, healthy habits to implement.

Control the Mind

We destroy every proud obstacle that keeps people from
knowing God. We capture their rebellious thoughts and
teach them to obey Christ.

2 CORINTHIANS 10:5 NLT

When I was compulsively drinking, I let the chips fall
wherever they may. Something, usually fear or worry, would
suddenly creep up on me, and I was powerless to stop the
troublesome thought or feeling from becoming the catalyst
for a flood of other bleak thoughts and ideas. Intense
feelings can result in irrational, extreme behaviors, and the
wreckage can extend far beyond mere mental distractions.
Left unchecked, upsetting emotions can bring disruptions
that lead to actions—more commonly, *reactions*. Knee-jerk
responses birthed from intense emotional states are rarely
helpful or productive. A new mindset is crucial to staying
ahead of the temptation to succumb to addictive drives.
We must control the mind before it takes over control of
the body to prevent regrettable decisions and undesirable
consequences. Taking each thought captive is critical
prevention against sin and remorse.

Surrender

Today I will identify negative thoughts and beliefs that have
led to upsetting emotions or actions I later regretted.

Sober Minded

Be sober, be vigilant; because your adversary the devil walks about like a roaring lion, seeking whom he may devour.

1 PETER 5:8 NKJV

Let me introduce you to your prime adversary: the devil. Oh, and don't forget his legion of demons. He is an often-present foe who requires just enough attention—but not too much. He would love for us to ignore him, let our defenses down, and fall blindly into one of his plentiful traps. Most people are blissfully clueless to the supernatural kingdom of darkness and its very real and destructive agenda. Start each day with a prayer of protection against dark forces and ask God to illuminate spiritual darkness with his holy light. Now for the good news: Jesus outranks the devil, so put your faith in his power to fight every battle alongside you. When you walk in obedience, Jesus faithfully guides every step and helps you steer clear of the devil's landmines.

Surrender

Today I will make a list of how I have given the devil a foothold, and I will repent.

Temptation Awaits

No temptation has overtaken you except what is common to mankind. And God is faithful; he will not let you be tempted beyond what you can bear. But when you are tempted, he will also provide a way out so that you can endure it.

1 CORINTHIANS 10:13 NIV

Over ten years ago, I made a decision that I didn't realize would carry devastating consequences. Though I felt trepidation and conviction all the way, I went ahead and acted on a desire to settle the score with someone else. Stone-cold sober at the time, I had no one to blame but myself. To say "the devil made me do it" would not even be accurate because he was not my deceiver that time. Literally minutes before I made this life-changing decision, my phone rang. It was a dear friend of mine, a pastor, a man of God. His name flashed on my phone's display, and in a fraction of a second, I dismissed God's lifeline. He would later say he felt led to reach out to me at that moment. God usually won't override our free will but promises to provide a way out when we are tempted. I rejected the escape hatch and had to pay the consequences.

Surrender

Today when I feel uncertainty or shame, I will ask Jesus for strength to resist temptation.

Mental Recalibration

Do not conform to the pattern of this world, but be transformed by the renewing of your mind. Then you will be able to test and approve what God's will is—his good, pleasing and perfect will.

ROMANS 12:2 NIV

It may seem like quitting addictive behaviors and walking with Jesus is the perfect prescription for a pain-free life, but that's not how it works. Though I was instantly freed of the urge to drink after a sincere prayer of repentance, I remained broken in other ways. Leaving alcohol behind was just the beginning of my journey to wholeness. The moment we completely surrender to the will of God, the messy road to sanctification begins. To *repent* means to turn away from the old, sinful life and toward the way of Jesus, and that means everything—including our thoughts. When I wake up saddled with a depressing outlook or negative thoughts, I battle the desire to stay in bed through a deliberate pursuit of praise and worship. The Lord inhabits the praises of his people, so start with a grateful attitude, and God will meet you there.

Surrender

Today I will remain aware of my mood, and if I feel unwanted emotions, I will ask God for help and motivation.

Place God First

"You must not have any other god but me."

EXODUS 20:3 NLT

Old Testament practices of idol worship and bowing down before gods may seem ancient and irrelevant, but are they truly so far from reality today? Addiction is the ultimate form of idolatry, as active addicts give their drug of choice priority over everything. Americans today submit to many gods: money, self, pleasure, drugs, work, even their spouses. When I married in 2004, I'd been sober for over a year and felt stable, but soon my husband became my new addiction. As a young newlywed, I was so enamored with him that God shifted to second place. I'd later learn the hard way that elevating a person to the status of a deity is extremely dangerous indeed. To become dependent upon a relationship, job, possession, or experience to gain security, purpose, or fulfillment is a recipe for disaster. Even the most rock-solid and devout human being is fallible. Learn to trust and have faith in God alone. He deserves nothing less than first place.

Surrender

Today I will focus on seeking God first in all areas of my life.

Seek His Guidance

"Cursed is the man who trusts in man and makes flesh his strength, whose heart turns away from the LORD."

JEREMIAH 17:5 ESV

My first attempt at sobriety was all backward. Desperate for answers, I frantically sought the world's offerings: outpatient treatment, AA groups, self-help books, and medications. Nothing I investigated was inherently bad but putting them before God was. Because I refused to acknowledge my Lord and Savior first, everything ultimately failed, and after brief stints of sobriety, another relapse always lurked around the corner. The first time I read today's verse, it blew my mind. The prophet Jeremiah wrote that we are cursed when we seek answers from people instead of from God. This does not mean that we don't need or benefit from the wise counsel of other Christians or professionals. But we should pursue God first. We honor him when we seek his guidance, and in turn, he will bless our obedience and faithfully open the right doors.

Surrender

Today I will remain fully aware of my tendency to seek earthly things before seeking God.

Fully Submit

"You meant evil against me; but God meant it for good,
in order to bring it about as it is this day,
to save many people alive."

GENESIS 50:20 NKJV

Partying in true Prince fashion, my 1999 kicked off with a drunk driving arrest instead of a bright harbinger of fun. But my run-in with law enforcement failed to serve as an enduring wake-up call. Just months later, I became a repeat offender after rear-ending a lady while I was in a drunken stupor. God didn't waste my mistake though. Instead, he used it to press pause on my recklessness, forcing me to seriously evaluate the trajectory of my life. The woman I had crashed into later breathed fresh hope into my situation by offering grace and forgiveness. Suddenly I grasped the possibility that maybe I *could* stop drinking. An eighteen-month break from booze didn't bring complete freedom, though clarity of mind and promptings of the Holy Spirit began to get my attention. Most importantly, God performed a great refining work and revealed the temporary nature of any recovery effort not driven by him. When fully submitted, even our bad decisions can be redeemed.

Surrender

Today I will lay all of my mistakes at the feet of Jesus.

Expect Trouble

"I have told you all this so that you may have peace in me.
Here on earth you will have many trials and sorrows.
But take heart, because I have overcome the world."

JOHN 16:33 NLT

After the Lord delivered me of all addictions in 2003,
I wore rose-colored glasses for many years. Although I
expected some hardship, I was completely blind to the
fact that my marriage was heading for catastrophe. One
afternoon while floundering in a pit of despair, I stumbled
upon John 16:33, and truth from the lips of Jesus restored
my sanity. Praise the Lord that my marriage survived and
that I was spared urges to drink in the process. Sober or not,
life on earth is no easy ride. God never wastes seasons of
trouble, always using trials to draw willing hearts closer to
him. Let the truth of John 16:33 sink deep into your soul.
God is the only way to peace. No matter what may happen
on this earthly journey, Jesus has conquered it all. That's a
promise you can trust with your life.

Surrender

Today I will rise above my circumstances and remember
that Jesus intimately understands every trouble I face.

Next Right Thing

Trust in the LORD with all your heart and lean not on your own understanding; in all your ways submit to him, and he will make your paths straight.

PROVERBS 3:5–6 NIV

Life is often overwhelming, and the tendency to avoid, procrastinate, or isolate may consume us. As a kid, I was a night owl who adored staying up late watching television when I was supposed to be doing homework or sleeping. In the moment, it was fun, but the next morning, I was tired, frazzled, and unprepared. It's the same for adults sometimes. We go for the pleasant stuff first and delay the things that require our immediate attention. But we can save ourselves a ton of unnecessary stress and misery simply by doing the next right thing. Whenever you are feeling unmotivated, depressed, or uncertain, ask God to show you what to do next and faithfully follow through.

Surrender

Today I will stay in the moment with God and ask him to guide my path.

Do Not Be Afraid

"The Lord is my helper; I will not be afraid.
What can mere mortals do to me?"

HEBREWS 13:6 NIV

Habitual binge drinking brought a constant state of
terror. I lived in fear of being "found out." I faced financial
uncertainty and worried about getting fired from my job. My
most familiar demon was panicking about the things I did
while blackout drunk. The worry of exposure plagued me
day and night, and I scrambled to cover my tracks so that my
shaky reputation wouldn't be soiled further. Even walking
into an AA meeting filled me with the intense fear that
someone would recognize me, exposing my dirty secret. Like
a hungry beast, agreeing with the devil's lies invites more
domination and control. Coming clean about your sin and
trusting God to handle the fallout is incredibly freeing. You'll
never regret doing the right thing, and your Helper will be
with you every step of the way.

Surrender

Today I lay all my fears at the foot of the cross of Christ and
trust him to protect me from my enemies.

Suit Up and Show Up

Our struggle is not against flesh and blood,
but against the rulers, against the authorities,
against the powers of this dark world and against
the spiritual forces of evil in the heavenly realms.

EPHESIANS 6:12 NIV

Many people spend extensive energy dwelling on past hurts, unexpected circumstances, and painful regrets. A victim mentality will darken the mind, rendering us ineffective for God. Disappointments and unmet expectations simply camouflage the real threat: the kingdom of darkness governed by the devil. Each day, ask Jesus to open your eyes to the battle in the supernatural realm and to show you how to fight. Then equip yourself with the full armor of God to stand strong against the Enemy. Keep the supernatural realm in proper perspective by giving it just the right amount of attention—not too much, not too little. Keep your eyes firmly on Jesus and his supreme authority as you battle with demons.

Surrender

Today I put on the full armor of God and ask Jesus to open
my eyes to the forces of darkness.

Bring Your Brokenness

We know that God causes everything to work together for
the good of those who love God and are called according to
his purpose for them.

ROMANS 8:28 NLT

Most addicts have assembled a treasury of wasted years—
time spent drunk, high, seeking a fix, or trying to recover.
Once sober, it's normal to think about the past as a whole lot
of wasted time. Maybe you've missed milestones, squandered
opportunities, or can't overcome thoughts of what could
have been. Let me encourage you! It's not too late to dedicate
the rest of your life to absolute service to God. All it takes is
a sincere desire to take every bit of the broken past—every
hurt, lost moment, and forsaken opportunity—and give it
to Jesus. He promises to make something beautiful from all
the shattered pieces and to use the rest of your life for his
purposes.

Surrender

Today I will stop dwelling on past regrets, and I will trust
God to make something beautiful from my mistakes.

Follow the Leader

If you confess with your mouth the Lord Jesus and believe in your heart that God has raised Him from the dead, you will be saved.

ROMANS 10:9 NKJV

Eschatology, soteriology, end times, pre- or post-tribulation? With so many denominations, biblical interpretations, and ideas about how the story of the Bible is playing out today, it is easy to feel confused and overwhelmed. Thankfully, the apostle Paul spelled it out very plainly for us in the book of Romans: just declare Jesus is Lord, believe in him, and follow his ways. No fancy training, research, or credentials are needed to surrender your life to Jesus. Simply declare him King and believe God raised him from the dead. That is all it takes for a transformation to start. Repent of your sins and ask for a new heart, one that is tender and willing to serve. A genuine expression of faith will lead to a changed life and the desire to follow the commands of Jesus.

Surrender

Today I will share the simple message of the gospel with someone else.

Hold On Tight

Moses answered the people, "Do not be afraid. Stand firm
and you will see the deliverance the LORD will bring you
today. The Egyptians you see today you will never see again."

EXODUS 14:13 NIV

Sometimes it's a fight to hold your head up. Unexpected
things happen, and something as common as a sick child
is enough to disrupt an otherwise normal routine. My
daughter once missed the bus, so I had to drive her to
school in a snowstorm, and on the way home, I got stuck
in a snowbank. We all have days that will push our buttons,
frazzle our nerves, and test our limits. The trick is to
minimize the damage, focus on gratitude, and seek God
right in the middle of the disruptions and stress. Every once
in a while, it's okay to just remain steady, to rest, and to not
make progress toward your goals. Hold tight, trust in the
Lord, and avoid making a bad situation worse.

Surrender

Today I will remember to breathe and ask God for help in
each moment, particularly during stressful situations.

Cause for Celebration

There is therefore now no condemnation
for those who are in Christ Jesus.

ROMANS 8:1 ESV

After we are delivered from addiction, the Enemy will
work tirelessly to keep us tethered to upsetting memories
of our old, sinful ways. It is often a delicate balance to
embrace a new life in Christ while still cleaning up old
wreckage. Regaining the trust of others takes patience and
perseverance. We will need to prove ourselves to some, and
those close to us might expect to see consistency from us
before believing our changes are genuine. But wallowing in
shame or beating ourselves up is unnecessary and unhelpful.
We have been changed by the power of the Holy Spirit, so it's
okay to feel joy even while dealing with past mistakes. Jesus
paid for every sin—past, present, and future—and that's
cause for celebration! His commands are not burdensome,
and he isn't asking for the moon, just simple repentance and
a desire to obey.

Surrender

Today I surrender every part of my past to the care of Jesus,
and I will remember that he took my shame and mistakes to
the cross.

Carry Your Cross

"If anyone would come after me,
let him deny himself and take up his cross
and follow me."

MATTHEW 16:24 ESV

Recovered addicts are some of the strongest, most resilient people around. When I was actively drinking, I could power through a hangover like nobody's business, but faking normalcy took a great deal of energy. Some addicts are expert drug dealers, hustlers, master manipulators, and con artists. Once we are finally free to channel addictive drives into positive outlets, we become unstoppable vessels for the Lord. Dying to self and offering Jesus complete access to our lives changes everything. Through trusting him, we can escape the nightmare of addiction with resiliency far exceeding that of the average person. Glorify God by using your gifts, talents, and grit for the kingdom.

Surrender

Today I will ask God to use my life as a living sacrifice.

Unchanging Truth

"What is truth?" Pilate asked. Then he went out again to the people and told them, "He is not guilty of any crime."

JOHN 18:38 NLT

When I was actively addicted, I clung to the shifting sands of emotions, culture, and the moods of others for guidance. I searched all around for meaning and identity, but the rules of my environment were constantly changing. As the world slips further into demonic deception, people seek to dismantle truth by denying its exclusivity. Author and apologist Frank Turek wrote, "Contrary *beliefs* are possible, but contrary *truths* are not possible."[1] There is only one true way to heaven and one influencer worth following, and his name is Jesus. Culture cannot be our bedrock. We need a stable, unchanging compass for guidance. We need God. Whenever you're confused, disturbed, or anxious, press into the Word of God and listen for the voice of the Holy Spirit. His truth never changes.

Surrender

Today I will rely on the unwavering truth found only in the presence of the Holy Trinity and the Word of God.

---

1   Norman Geisler and Frank Turek, *I Don't Have Enough Faith to Be an Atheist* (Wheaton, IL: Crossway Books, 2004), 38. See also Turek's website www.crossexamined.org for helpful resources.

Life Assurance

Jesus said to him, "I am the way, and the truth, and the life.
No one comes to the Father except through me."

JOHN 14:6 ESV

Active addiction tends to block our minds from thinking about the future because our top priority is surviving the day. But recovery brings a fresh wake-up call to the reality that we need to protect our assets. Instead of living in the moment, we begin wondering if retirement is even possible and considering those whom we will leave behind when we pass from this world. But as we're haggling over term or whole life insurance, death benefits, and cash values, we need to remember that everything on earth is temporary. Financial planning is important and will help relieve stress about the unknown, but we can find total assurance and everlasting life only in Jesus.

Surrender

Today I will ask Jesus to help me stay focused on eternity as I navigate my earthly journey.

He Sees You

Hagar used another name to refer to the LORD, who had spoken to her. She said, "You are the God who sees me." She also said, "Have I truly seen the One who sees me?"

GENESIS 16:13 NLT

Because of my fragile sense of identity, mirrors were some of my best friends as a teenager. I'd gaze into any available reflective surface just to make sure I existed, later finding temporary acceptance in fleeting relationships, keg parties, and the brief recognition that came from my job as a small-market television news anchor. Once I sought God and was delivered of addiction, I realized my flimsy secular substitutes could never satisfy my deep need to be seen. My quest for external validation was replaced by an intense desire to know Jesus. In good times and in bad, when you're feeling alone and unappreciated, remember that God's eyes will never leave you, not even for a moment.

Surrender

Today I will remember that I am never out of God's sight. He loves me like no one else can.

Seek the Source

"Let me have silence, and I will speak,
and let come on me what may."

JOB 13:13 ESV

Because of Jesus, we have an open door to the presence of God. Do you realize how amazing that is? We don't need fancy rites, rituals, or ceremonies, no blood sacrifices, long prayers, or appointments. God Almighty is ready and waiting to speak to you anytime, anywhere. Nothing is more important than learning to hear God speak to your very own heart. Most of us dwell within an exhausting rat race of distractions, and the still, small voice of Jesus won't fight through chaos. Discipline yourself to find quiet space within the cares of life, whether it's thirty seconds, five minutes, or five hours. Bring all your praises, cares, worries, and petitions, and practice sitting quietly in his presence. He will speak if you are willing to listen.

Surrender

Today I will spend quiet time at the feet of Jesus, thanking, praising, and sharing my concerns.

The Way of Peace

*This is the confidence that we have toward him,
that if we ask anything according to his will he hears us.*

1 JOHN 5:14 ESV

Living outside of God's will created a life of endless chaos for me. I made major life decisions impulsively and pursued my own interests, goals, and pleasures. My frantic desire to avoid being alone repeatedly drove me into the wrong relationships. Jesus was simply a figure of old, and the Bible was an irrelevant book taking up space and collecting dust on my bookshelf. Deep in my addiction, my prayers were crisis-oriented: *God, please get me out of this* or *Please let me make it home without getting arrested.* I never bothered to ask God what was best for my life or to seek his will. When I finally surrendered and made Jesus my Lord, life took on incredible meaning and purpose, and I was finally able to experience the peace that surpasses all understanding.

Surrender

Today I will seek God's perfect will in each moment and
wait for his guidance.

No Substitutes

Seek the LORD and his strength;
seek his presence continually!
1 CHRONICLES 16:11 ESV

The search for meaning draws many to New Age teachings and the empty promises of self-promotion, happiness, and material success. Thought gurus and prosperity gospel pastors preach blasphemies about thinking things into being and attracting possessions, people, and situations. These fairy tales are directly opposed to biblical teachings. In the book of Romans, Paul urges followers to abandon empty worldly pursuits to seek Jesus—the true source of all wisdom and power. Transformation begins with turning from trends, fads, and fallible people to the Lord. Humble obedience will bring rock-solid assurance of his ability to meet every need. The world and its candy-coated allure will fade as we seek true nourishment.

Surrender

Today I will repent and change from my old, self-directed
thinking to trusting Jesus completely.

First Prize

Do you not know that in a race all the runners run, but only one gets the prize? Run in such a way as to get the prize.

1 CORINTHIANS 9:24 NIV

Exercise was something I completely avoided until I was thirty. Keeping my demons in check was enough of a workout, and navigating the workday consumed all the energy I could muster. But when I was delivered of addiction, I fell in love with running and began to experience great joy in working for a natural reward. The Holy Spirit even began to speak to me during workout time. I have received some of my best writing ideas while working out. Leisure activities and hobbies can become God-honoring when we do them exclusively for his glory, and he often blesses us during these times if our hearts remain free of self-promotion. Instead of trying to win a physical prize or award, I devote this time to God. Having a healthy body enables us to better serve him.

Surrender

Today I will use my body in a way that honors God, and I will reflect on the joy that awaits with Jesus after I complete this earthly race.

What Would Jesus Do?

Godliness with contentment is great gain.

1 TIMOTHY 6:6 ESV

My deepest desire is to live a God-honoring life, one that makes Jesus proud. When I sit down to watch a television show or engage in a conversation with a coworker, the first thought that comes to mind is, *Would Jesus approve?* I imagine him right beside me at all times as I pray for help with weeding out unfruitful pursuits or activities. As we grow in relationship with God, our tastes will change, naturally moving us toward purer pursuits. As we seek his face in all things, the struggle and frustration that comes from pushing our own agendas will begin to fade. Allowing God to take the driver's seat is liberating. We no longer strive to figure things out or to control outcomes. It is so much easier and more peaceful to seek the way of Jesus.

Surrender

Today I will ask God to remove anything from my life that does not honor him or wasn't his idea.

Grasp Goodness

Temptation comes from our own desires,
which entice us and drag us away.

JAMES 1:14 NLT

The wicked world doesn't disappear because we become miserable enough to repent of our addictions and come to faith in Jesus. Temptation still awaits around every corner, and the devil steps up his attacks once we are set on fire for God. So many sin opportunities emerge daily—maybe a temptation to gossip, waste time, or overreact. But we always have a choice and the Holy Spirit to guide us in all truth. A safe and temptation-free life isn't going to happen, but God will faithfully counteract each landmine with a wholesome escape. We alone decide whether to sin, and our disobedience will bring consequences.

Surrender

Today I pray Jesus will protect me from temptation and
from the lies of the devil.

Suffering Is Christlike

Since therefore Christ suffered in the flesh, arm yourselves with the same way of thinking, for whoever has suffered in the flesh has ceased from sin.

1 PETER 4:1 ESV

Getting high on life can be exhilarating, and many believe their problems are long gone once the drugs disappear from their life. And who doesn't desire a pain-free existence filled with joy and abundance? At first, I thought sobriety would produce nonstop blessings, but I was in for a rude awakening when I encountered a real trial outside of my addiction. It was then that I discovered that achieving sobriety and radical freedom from addiction did not mean that I would be free from ever suffering on earth again. It's a scary thing to discover that life will always have its pains, but we don't need to be afraid. Enduring pain and hardship actually brings us closer to Christ, offering just a tiny taste of his sacrifice on the cross. We bring honor to his name when we faithfully seek him during times of trial.

Surrender

Today I will remember to seek God even more faithfully when I am experiencing pain or hardship.

Lies Multiply

Jesus answered them, "Truly, truly, I say to you,
everyone who practices sin is a slave to sin."

JOHN 8:34 ESV

Telling lies terrified me as a child. But years later, alcohol
allowed deception to roll from my mouth like water
off a duck's back. As I fudged the truth, I became more
comfortable with my lack of integrity. The discrepancies
grew between my true self and the one I'd adopted for the
world, and my tolerance for lies and sin increased. Getting
away with something can be powerfully reinforcing,
furthering the idea that increasing levels of disobedience
are no big deal. Every time I drove home drunk without
consequence, my willingness to break the law grew stronger.
But no wrongdoing is hidden from God. We will be held
accountable—either in this life or in the next—for every
word we speak and action we take.

Surrender

Today I will repent of lies, strive to be truthful to myself and
others, and honor God with my choices.

The Power of Choice

We are debtors, not to the flesh,
to live according to the flesh.

ROMANS 8:12 ESV

The first time I got drunk, I knew exactly what I was doing. Years of watching my parents and other family members come under the influence of alcohol convinced me I was going to love drinking. The night that alcohol and I met was so powerfully reinforcing that I quickly made the decision to seek intoxication as often as possible. Addicted people usually have many reasons to justify their behavior, and some are legitimate. A dysfunctional home, trauma, or loneliness can make abusing drugs and alcohol or wasting hours at a slot machine seem to be the only solution. But mind-altering substances and behaviors can squelch the Holy Spirit and stifle the voice of God, and he will not compete with an idol for first place in our lives.

Surrender

Today I will choose to honor Jesus rather than to satisfy my flesh. I will ask him to help me make decisions that glorify him.

Count the Cost

Do not look at wine when it is red,
when it sparkles in the cup and goes down smoothly.

PROVERBS 23:31 ESV

That first sip of beer was always so good. The first can was delicious, too, and sometimes even the entire six pack. Even if the night ended in a blackout, shameful behavior, or another consequence, my mind's eye would transport me back to the first few moments of pleasure. It's called *euphoric recall* in the world of addiction. But the short-term bliss always spun like a boomerang, with that initial glorious taste quickly spiraling into shame and remorse. The Enemy loves to magnify the brief excitement that comes with a taste of sin, but the total picture is one of utter devastation. When we weigh the entire cost, the price to mind, body, and soul is much too high to justify.

Surrender

Today I will reflect upon the total cost of my addiction and the disaster it has caused. I will thank Jesus for delivering me.

Going to Extremes

Be not among drunkards
or among gluttonous eaters of meat.

PROVERBS 23:20 ESV

Our dopamine-driven society of excess is always seeking the next big thing. A world filled with plentiful distractions and opportunities makes it easy to numb ourselves with television, sex, food, and addictions of all kinds. Many struggle with moderation in just about everything. We are the society of *more*, craving attention, stimulation, and entertainment. The quest for satisfaction through earthly things is an unquenchable fire that alienates us from God and drives people to depend on substances and objects to cope. When we are distracted by worldly pursuits, we cannot hear his voice. Seek God-approved enjoyment and entertainment and avoid excess in all things.

Surrender

Today I will be satisfied with the simple things and the joy of knowing I have eternal life in Jesus.

February

Take the Plunge

"When they bring you before the synagogues and the rulers
and the authorities, do not be anxious about how you should
defend yourself or what you should say, for the Holy Spirit
will teach you in that very hour what you ought to say."

LUKE 12:11–12 ESV

Over-preparing and stressing about every public
appearance or live interview was a bad habit I struggled
to overcome. Jotting down ideas as bullet points is fine,
but pasting notes all over the computer while my palms
dripped with sweat showed a lack of trust in God. Do you
have enough faith to let the Holy Spirit take over? Tuning
in to his voice invites his marvelous presence, and stepping
out in faith enables your Creator to work within you for his
glory. Move aside and trust God to take over. As you learn
to trust and take greater risks, you will begin to see just how
faithfully he will meet you.

Surrender

Today I will do my part and then surrender the rest to God,
inviting the Holy Spirit to guide, direct, and lead.

Pick Your Battles

Though we walk in the flesh, we do not wage battle
according to the flesh, for the weapons of our warfare
are not of the flesh, but divinely powerful for the destruction
of fortresses.

2 CORINTHIANS 10:3–4 NASB

The flesh constantly beckons with opportunities to sin, and
the devil wages war in our minds. Years ago, I had no idea
that most of my thoughts were fueled by the devil. Cravings
for alcohol dominated my mind. I lived in fear of rejection
from people, and a steady stream of validation from others
seemed the only way to survive. Fighting our human nature
without Jesus is a losing battle. Once he is in the driver's seat,
we become aware that the Enemy is the source of deception,
temptation, and strongholds. He is the Father of Lies and
wants to block the great power available to us in Christ.
Once we become aware of our God-given authority, we have
the necessary weapons to rebuke and defeat the devil.

Surrender

Today I will ask Jesus to search me and expose
any wrong thinking.

Sin Bites

I do not understand what I do.
For what I want to do I do not do,
but what I hate I do.

ROMANS 7:15 NIV

As a teenager, I led two lives. During the week, I was a studious bookworm, but come Friday, I was hellbent on finding the next gravel pit party. Though each gathering brought initial excitement, every hungover morning was the same—paralyzing shame and regret and promises to swear off alcohol. With Jesus, we are freed from self-hatred. Though we may continue to stumble into sin, God's plan for us to grow in sanctification finally becomes clear. When we are Spirit-filled, disobedience feels awful, but repentance brings forgiveness. Thank God we have a Savior whose blood covers every mistake.

Surrender

Today I seek to love the ways of Jesus and to walk in them.

Be Discerning

"The thief comes only to steal and kill and destroy;
I have come that they may have life, and have it to the full."

JOHN 10:10 NIV

Two opposing forces are warring for your soul. One is the beautiful and Holy God of the Bible, and the other is a counterfeit being disguised as an angel of light. The dark force will offer attractive alternatives to righteous living: a significant other, a business opportunity, or something else that, on the surface, looks really good. The devil knows how to artfully entice through a pretty little package, smooth talk, or empty promises that initially sound appealing. Though we shouldn't hyperfocus on the Enemy, we must exercise caution about his schemes and his desire to lead us into temptation. Vigilantly guard your thoughts, seek God through prayer and the Bible, and recognize how "little" sins give the destroyer easy access. Pursue God and you will be spared much misery.

Surrender

Today I will intentionally pursue Jesus and will avoid temptation by staying away from things that displease God.

Abide in Him

I am the vine, ye are the branches:
He that abideth in me, and I in him,
the same beareth much fruit.

JOHN 15:5 ASV

Our culture promotes independence, autonomy, and the false idea that creating a fulfilling life is possible without God. The Bible says otherwise. Jesus is the very breath that keeps our bodies going. He enables every heartbeat. When we strive to do things without him, we move outside the safety of his will. Sometimes our efforts might even seem to work, but anything generated without God's approval will eventually fail or cause much heartache and frustration. The true blessings that come from godly living remain out of reach when we deny our need for the Savior. He desires to lead us into a life filled with promise and purpose, but this amazing reality requires surrender and a willing heart.

Surrender

Today I will remember to make prayer a regular part of my day, seeking God in all things.

Today Is the Day

The LORD replied: "Write down the revelation and make it plain on tablets so that a herald may run with it."

HABAKKUK 2:2 NIV

Habakkuk was an Old Testament prophet given the task of delivering to God's wayward people an ominous warning about their impending Babylonian captivity. Habakkuk's message needed to carry a sense of urgency. He needed the people to understand it and respond quickly. The bottom line: the people needed to change their ways and fast. Many who are battling addictions or enjoying a lifestyle of debauchery make excuses and promise to abandon their wicked ways sometime later. *Quitting is too hard in summer. I'm going through a lot of stress at work. Life is too boring without it. I'll start after the holidays.* I told myself all these lies and more. Delaying what's necessary for righteous living keeps us ensnared and allows our addiction to grow deeper roots. Every day in bondage gives the Enemy more ground. Decide today to run toward a new life in Jesus.

Surrender

Today I will ask God to help me take action to change patterns of behavior that are hindering me.

Light Up My Life

Immediately, something like scales fell from Saul's eyes,
and he could see again. He got up and was baptized.

ACTS 9:18 NIV

I spent fifteen years with blinders on, trapped in a cycle
of blackout binge drinking. Satan had deceived me into
believing I could somehow morph into a social drinker,
which perpetuated a cycle of constant relapse. Instead of me
becoming like the normal people I envied, every attempt to
consume alcohol responsibly only ended with deep shame
and regret. The answer had to begin with an intrinsic desire
to turn from my destructive path, and Jesus allowed me to
experience much pain and misery before I became desperate
enough to embrace the true answer. When I finally cried out
in surrender, I was able to leave my life of addiction at the
foot of the cross.

Surrender

Today I pray God will open my eyes to the root of my
problems and show me the way out.

Trust His Timing

Blessed is the one who perseveres under trial because,
having stood the test, that person will receive the crown
of life that the Lord has promised to those who love him.

JAMES 1:12 NIV

I stumbled upon this verse in a hotel room during a very low point in my marriage. My husband and I had agreed to separate briefly and were taking turns going from our home to the hotel. Alone one night, I picked up the Bible for the first time in a long while. A random sweep of the book of James made this verse jump from the page, leading me to believe the Scripture verse was a sign from God indicating my struggle would soon end with a beautiful reconciliation. Little did I know that the Lord had much more to teach me, and the long road to overcoming would last a year and a half. In times of trial, we must avoid putting Jesus on a schedule. He knows what we need, and he longs for us to rest in his presence while he teaches and refines us. We can trust that the time we spend waiting on him is never wasted.

Surrender

Today I will remember that God's timing is always perfect, and I will ask him what he wants to teach me while I wait.

Never Too Late

> To Him who is able to do exceedingly abundantly above all
> that we ask or think, according to the power that works in
> us, to Him be glory.

EPHESIANS 3:20–21 NKJV

The Enemy loves to highlight the mistakes we have made and the time we have wasted. He reminds us of all the missed opportunities, failed relationships, things we can't change, and shameful stuff we did while drunk or high. He whispers, *Just keep on drinking and using. Your life is a mess and can't be fixed. You're old. You're washed up. It's too late. Why not forget about everything for a while?* My father was so deep into alcohol addiction and chronic health problems that he had lost sight of his identity in Jesus, and the Enemy's murmurings eventually silenced the voice of reason. The devil is a liar. It's not too late! God can do more with a fully surrendered life than you could ever imagine. Submit to him and buckle up because you're in for the ride of your life. Jesus has an amazing way of redeeming lost time.

Surrender

Today I fully surrender my life and my will to God.

Don't Panic

Let him ask in faith, with no doubting, for he who doubts
is like a wave of the sea driven and tossed by the wind.

JAMES 1:6 NKJV

A brand-new life in sobriety promised smooth sailing ahead, but I didn't know the most painful trial of my life was coming. As I've previously mentioned, after seven years of marriage, a massive catastrophe almost destroyed my relationship. Crying out to God didn't seem to help, and I felt stuck in a vortex and unable to hear his voice. After a year and a half of brokenness, my husband and I finally realized the impossibility of fixing things alone, and our surrender birthed a miracle. I finally believed the gentle voice I'd heard speaking into my low moments of crumbling faith, the still, small whisperings of the Holy Spirit to trust God and find peace in the storm. My heart soared when I embraced the truth. Peace will come like a river when we seek Jesus in desperation and put our trust in him.

Surrender

Today I ask the Lord to grow my faith, guide and direct me, and bring me to people and places that offer the right kind of help.

Let Go and Let God

The man said, "Let me go, for the dawn is breaking!"
But Jacob said, "I will not let you go unless you bless me."

GENESIS 32:26 NLT

The book of Genesis details Jacob wrestling until daybreak with a man who later is revealed as the Angel of the Lord—the preincarnate Christ. As dawn breaks, Jacob utters an exasperated cry, "I will not let you go unless you bless me!" God can handle our doubts, demands, and defiance, but fighting his will is a losing battle. After fifteen years of alcohol addiction and endless exhausting attempts to force my growing problem into submission, I failed to accomplish the goal of responsible drinking. Each relapse left me bloodied and battle worn as God waited nearby. Jesus wants nothing more from us than to walk in close communion with him and to surrender our will to his lordship. When we become willing to let go, we can finally stop striving and rest in total confidence with him.

Surrender

Today I surrender everything to Jesus, especially the situations and people I have been trying to fix.

All the Way

God is working in you, giving you the desire
and the power to do what pleases him.

PHILIPPIANS 2:13 NLT

God is working within us long before we cry out to him.
Isn't that amazing? He is intentionally molding our hearts,
using our wrong choices to exert gentle pressure, and
aligning our will with his. The journey to sanctification is a
life-long process, with the goal to become more Christlike
every day. As you grow, develop, and increase in obedience,
you'll become attuned to his true call for your life, no longer
living frustrated and puzzled. As God begins to faithfully
open doors, your faith and trust will increase. Our lives are
his. Ask him to open the path before you, step by step. He is
faithful to do so.

Surrender

Today I am grateful that I am a work in progress and that I
can trust God to never give up on me.

Who's on First?

"I am the Alpha and the Omega," says the Lord God,
"who is, and who was, and who is to come, the Almighty."

REVELATION 1:8 NIV

How much of your time is spent in close intimacy with Jesus? Our self-driven culture and its pleasures call to the flesh through food, drinks, and experiences that push God to the back burner. Without a kingdom mindset, we simply move from one dopamine hit to the next. This world and its carnal delicacies will pass away, so we must be careful not to spend our precious years consumed by the world. God doesn't want scraps or castoffs. So shut off your phone, log out of social media, and get into the Word. Seriously evaluate the amount of time you are devoting to prayer and Bible study, for God deserves your absolute best.

Surrender

Today I will be intentional about how I spend my time and
will focus on giving God my best.

Perfect Confidence

They said to the woman, "We no longer believe just because of what you said; now we have heard for ourselves, and we know that this man really is the Savior of the world."

JOHN 4:42 NIV

Belief in Jesus Christ is the cornerstone of Christian faith and the only access point to God. Salvation, in a nutshell, is very simple: *believe* that Jesus is who he claims to be—that he died on the cross and rose again on the third day— and confess him as your personal Lord and Savior. True conversion will bring a sincere desire to repent and turn from sin, a hatred of disobedience, and a deep longing to spend eternity with God. The book of James teaches that faith and good works align, so Christianity naturally produces the desire to glorify God through righteous living (see 2:24). Walking with the Lord will be rich, full, and challenging, but everything begins with a simple, childlike faith in the God of all creation.

Surrender

Today I will believe the message of the gospel with childlike wonder.

Gather Together

*Let us consider…not giving up meeting together, as some are
in the habit of doing, but encouraging one another—
and all the more as you see the Day approaching.*

HEBREWS 10:24–25 NIV

COVID-19 wreaked havoc on the church, causing many houses of worship to shut down in response to fears propagated by the media. Though some continued to pursue workarounds through outdoor services and other alternative approaches to worship, many people grew terrified of human contact. Countless pastors encouraged folks to quarantine, causing tremendous spikes in addictions, mental illnesses, and suicide. While some with high-risk medical conditions had to be extra cautious, many healthy people resisted returning to church because they had grown comfortable watching worship services from home in their jammies. While the church is much more than a building, the Bible calls us to come together to worship our Holy God, to fellowship, to disciple, and to serve. Much of that can't be done from a couch. There is no substitute for gathering as a body of believers.

Surrender

Today I will remember the importance of gathering and won't make excuses to avoid church.

Ruler of All

[Christ is seated] far above all rule and authority,
power and dominion, and every name that is invoked,
not only in the present age but also in the one to come.

EPHESIANS 1:21 NIV

When we are children, our earthly father is often the
rule maker in the household, and we must submit to his
authority. I didn't endure frequent spankings as a kid
because the frightening crack of Dad's belt whipping from
its loops was enough. When we are adults, our employers
may become the chief authorities, and while most leaders
are fair, others are fear-producing dictators. We must obey
the laws of the land and respect positions of authority, but
each person also has an ultimate ruler. Maybe you're in an
oppressive situation at work, in a relationship, or even at
church. Take comfort in knowing there exists no higher
rank than that of Jesus Christ. Pray that he will begin to
take control of situations and people in your life, and always
remember that you must answer to him first.

Surrender

Today I recognize Jesus as my ultimate ruler, and I
surrender to his lordship.

Hope Springs Eternal

Faith is the assurance of things hoped for,
the conviction of things not seen.

HEBREWS 11:1 ESV

Hope springs eternal," wrote eighteenth century poet Alexander Pope, believing that people always wish for the best, even in the face of adversity. Life on earth can be a mixed bag. Sometimes we get exactly what we want, but then out of nowhere, tragedies or unmet expectations can leave us disappointed or even crushed. Maybe we wanted relationship restoration, but a divorce happened instead. Perhaps the prodigal child we've spent years praying for still has not returned, or we're struggling to barely make it through each day. Even in sobriety, we are not promised a picture-perfect existence filled with daisies and ice cream sundaes. This life is merely a staging site as we travel through to our eternal home. When we accept Jesus as Savior, we inherit heavenly rewards. When disappointments come, may we find comfort and rest in the eternal hope that awaits.

Surrender

Today I will place my hope in my eternal reward and not in my circumstances.

Fireproof Faith

Without faith it is impossible to please him,
for whoever would draw near to God must believe
that he exists and that he rewards those who seek him.

HEBREWS 11:6 ESV

Even though Jesus has delivered me from so much, my lack of faith can be downright embarrassing sometimes. My life's journey reveals countless examples of the Lord's guidance and protection—as well as many situations where I refused to wait on him. Looking at life in reverse can be extremely faith-building; hindsight often reveals the hand of God in all its glory. Sometimes we beg God to change people or situations, and later we see why they didn't work out. Things we wanted so badly may have been potential disasters that God's hand alone averted. As time passes, his reasons come into focus, and they are always for our greater good. As we trust Jesus, we experience the freedom and peace of believing he truly is in control.

Surrender

Today I will trust Jesus and have faith that he is working all things for my good.

Choose Life

The sin of this one man, Adam, caused death to rule over many. But even greater is God's wonderful grace and his gift of righteousness, for all who receive it will live in triumph over sin and death through this one man, Jesus Christ.

ROMANS 5:17 NLT

Experimentation with alcohol started innocently. I found acceptance and temporary belonging in a beer bottle, and an exciting, problem-free life seemed possible through the mask of intoxication. But I invited death each time I popped that longneck beer or took a swig from a 40-ounce malt liquor, and each drunken episode chipped away pieces of my soul. Addiction came on fast and steep, with the deception of drunkenness ushering in deeper levels of sin over time. A stunning realization dawned when I was twenty-eight: *You're not going to make it to thirty if you don't stop*. Two years later, I finally surrendered and repented. Sin leads to death, but there is life and freedom awaiting in Jesus Christ.

Surrender

Today I will remember that sinful behaviors will shorten my life and lead to death.

Bread from Heaven

Jesus answered, "It is written: 'Man shall not live on bread alone, but on every word that comes from the mouth of God.'"

MATTHEW 4:4 NIV

I received my first Bible in the third grade: a beautiful red leather book with *Melissa* stamped on the front in gold letters. I tucked it onto a bookshelf and never opened it. Today, Bible study is like breathing—required for my survival. Burying the truths of the Word of God deep in my heart offers protection and guidance. Being in the Bible every day is vital to our Christian walk, and God's love letter to us is definitely not something we can read once and stick on a shelf. As you pursue the heart of Jesus daily through this inspired work, you will see him speaking directly into relevant life situations, and the Bible will grow into the most exciting book you've ever known.

Surrender

Today I will dedicate time to studying the Word of God.

Remain Vigilant

Jesus said to him, "Away from me, Satan! For it is written:
'Worship the Lord your God, and serve him only.'"

MATTHEW 4:10 NIV

C. S. Lewis once wrote: "The safest road to Hell is the gradual one—the gentle slope, soft underfoot, without sudden turnings, without milestones, without signposts."[2] Firm resolve can easily slip in recovery, and complacency may lead to the deception that you've got everything mastered. After submitting to Jesus, expect the devil to step up his game. Crafty and cunning, he gains access in unexpected ways; perhaps he suggests frequenting bars again, leads you to believe gossiping is no big deal, or begins highlighting perceived slights from others. Before you know it, you're harboring resentment and trash-talking a coworker at the water cooler. Dabbling in sin gives Satan a foothold, so carefully guard your words and actions to remain vigilant in your walk with Jesus.

Surrender

Today I will ask Jesus to help me avoid traps set by
the Evil One.

---

2   C. S. Lewis, *The Screwtape Letters* (New York: HarperCollins
    Publishers, 2001), 61.

Living Word

The word of God is living and active, sharper than any two-edged sword, piercing to the division of soul and of spirit, of joints and of marrow, and discerning the thoughts and intentions of the heart.

HEBREWS 4:12 ESV

The Bible never called my name until I was well into my twenties and in full crisis mode. Just an antiquated book collecting dust, I searched the world over and came up empty before I was drawn to it. It is the most amazing and best-selling work in history, and the more we study it, the more it speaks. The Bible is a God-breathed manual for living, and daily immersion in God's Word is the most rewarding practice we can undertake. Through diligent study and journaling, your eyes will open to the many ways God uses his Word to speak to unique life situations. Recording answered prayers is also an incredible faith builder. The Bible is exciting and filled with action, mystery, and prophecy—concluding with Christ's stunning promise to return and reconcile heaven and earth to himself.

Surrender

Today I will ask Jesus to make me a lover of his Word and to help me prioritize time with him.

Man's Empty Praise

On the contrary, we speak as those approved by God to
be entrusted with the gospel. We are not trying to please
people but God, who tests our hearts.

1 THESSALONIANS 2:4 NIV

People couldn't get enough of my mother. A great
conversationalist and storyteller, she truly loved blessing
others with her time and attention. But my father's
alcoholism drove her into codependency, a behavior I
learned over the years. Being polite, avoiding conflict, and
making people happy seemed her way to avoid pain. As
a teen, I compromised myself to serve others, and soon
the deep desire to be liked began to take its toll. Needing
external validation is an endless, bloodsucking slog. Nothing
in the world will ever satisfy like Jesus can. Seeking the
approval of others to feel accepted will never bring long-
term fulfillment. Finding identity in Jesus Christ, the one
who made you, is the only way to fill the void within.

Surrender

Today I will focus only on pleasing God. I will ask him to
teach me his ways.

Jesus Paid It All

I can do all this through him
who gives me strength.
PHILIPPIANS 4:13 NIV

While Philippians 4:13 is an extremely popular verse among life coaches, motivational gurus, and self-help afficionados, these people often take it out of context. Well-intentioned people misuse and abuse this famous passage written by the apostle Paul, misinterpreting it to mean that Jesus will personally endorse their visions, dreams, and career aspirations. The book of Philippians is actually a prison epistle, written when Paul was very close to death. In this letter, Paul declares his belief that no trial of the world will come against the power of Jesus Christ. Oh, how the burdens of earth pale in comparison! We trivialize this verse when we make it about personal enrichment. Instead, we should ponder it with reverence, knowing Jesus is close in both our joy and our suffering.

Surrender

Today I will contemplate the incredible sacrifice of Jesus Christ and his journey to the cross.

Unwavering Faith

As it is written, "I have made you the father of many nations"—in the presence of the God in whom he believed, who gives life to the dead and calls into existence the things that do not exist.

ROMANS 4:17 ESV

Abraham never doubted God's promise. How about you? Have you struggled to hold on to a hope or dream? My seemingly perfect marriage hit the skids at year seven, and a painful eighteen-month separation followed. During that time, I went through a roller coaster of emotions. But the season in the wilderness brought me closer to God than ever, and at the end, he spoke a promise: *I will restore your marriage if you surrender it to me.* Whatever you're going through today, empty yourself, seek God's face, and trust him with the outcome.

Surrender

Today I will surrender everything to Jesus and will trust him with the process.

Look Deeper

As he thinketh in his heart, so is he: Eat and drink,
saith he to thee; but his heart is not with thee.

PROVERBS 23:7 KJV

As a new Christian, I was swayed by the desire to make a Bible verse mean something it really didn't. This particular passage has become a cornerstone "teaching" of the New Age movement, promising health and wealth through the power of thinking. A right mindset is important, but it's not an excuse to twist Bible verses. Rather than reference the power of positive thinking, this passage describes the fruit borne from the actions of a miserly man who does not truly want to offer his friend something to eat. The verse teaches the importance of evaluating whether a person's talk matches up with their life. Lip service not accompanied by a true desire to serve God and his people is pure hypocrisy. Look deeper into Scripture and ask the Holy Spirit to reveal its truth.

Surrender

Today I pray for discernment, wisdom, and the power of the
Holy Spirit to glean truth from the Bible.

True Vision

Where there is no vision, the people perish:
but he that keepeth the law, happy is he.

PROVERBS 29:18 KJV

During my dive into the New Age movement over twenty years ago, I was easily entranced by the popular trend of designing a vision board. Proponents of vision boards believe that highlighting future goals and desires and pasting them onto a poster to encourage attention and focus will "manifest" those goals. I didn't skimp on my art project, going all in with stickers, multicolored Sharpies, and bold word-of-faith proclamations. Some desires were physical, like a personal best in a foot race, and others were material, like that Tiffany bracelet I yearned to see dangling from my wrist. Though having goals is fine and good, the verse written by King Solomon isn't talking about personal success or enrichment. It is about receiving communication from *God*, not some New Age guru.

Surrender

Today I pray that God will make my path straight and will provide revelation through his inspired book—the Holy Bible.

Learn from Landmines

"After you have suffered a little while, the God of all grace, who has called you to his eternal glory in Christ, will himself restore, confirm, strengthen and establish you."

1 PETER 5:10 ESV

My parents never knew how to handle my dangerous experimentation with alcohol. One day after I had raided their liquor cabinet, they found me in a drunken stupor and decided to ship me off to spend the summer with my aunt. It actually turned out to be a pretty fun experience. Once back home, my little incident had been forgotten. But when my parents continued to bust me for drinking or sneaking out at night, I would use my top-notch manipulation tactics to persuade them to grant me an early release from their restrictions. My growing problem was buffered by my parents' failure to hold their boundaries. As adults, running from the consequences of our own choices can prevent God from instilling valuable life lessons. He can use our mistakes to initiate incredible growth experiences if we are patient.

Surrender

Today I will think about the impact of a sinful lifestyle.

March

Lead with Love

"My command is this:
Love each other as I have loved you."

JOHN 15:12 NIV

Our nation is more divided than ever. It's "us" versus "them." Kitchen tables have become battlegrounds, and holiday gatherings that were once joyful are now often tense. A close family member once revealed their decision to embrace a particular sinful lifestyle. The news hit me like a ton of bricks, and I sat in stunned silence trying to digest the shocking information. After a long pause, I stressed my Christian faith and my belief that this person's choices went against the teachings of Jesus. While I could not endorse or approve of the lifestyle, I reiterated my deep, profound love for my family member. We prayed and cried together and shared a healing conversation in which our main goal was to develop greater understanding.

Surrender

Today I will lead with love and seek to understand while
standing firm in my Christian values.

Sin Is Costly

The fear of the LORD adds length to life,
but the years of the wicked are cut short.

PROVERBS 10:27 NIV

Until I turned fifteen, I was a decent kid who obeyed my parents. But in the late 1980s, I gravitated toward a crowd of people who frequently broke rules and took risks. I soon began blackout binge drinking, and drunk driving quickly followed. In my desire to follow the crowd and to find a way to medicate my massive abandonment wound, I turned a blind eye to sin's slippery slope. Disobedience usually starts small and is often easily justified, but tolerance for doing the wrong things develops in the same way as it does for drugs, alcohol, or other addictions. Soon we are swallowing more sin and rationalizing it away while the Enemy rejoices. Every act that defies God comes at a price, with escalating costs the longer we dance with the devil.

Surrender

Today I will ask the Holy Spirit to bring conviction when I am tempted to sin, and I will quickly repent.

Stuck on Stupid

The way of a fool is right in his own eyes,
but a wise man listens to advice.

PROVERBS 12:15 ESV

Isolation is probably the biggest mistake a newly sober person can make, and it became a massive downfall during my first round of sobriety from 1999 to 2001. I casually attended AA meetings but stayed guarded and refused to let people into my life. Everyone needs support, preferably wise Christians who have similar life experiences and can be loving and truthful without judgment. During my eighteen months of mask-wearing, resentment built up inside me, and two years later, the bars beckoned. We need discipleship from more seasoned Christ followers in order to grow and to resist temptation. It's okay if AA doesn't fit. Just find at least one Bible-believer who is willing to become a mentor. Reveal the real you and be teachable. Deciding to act upon head chatter is a big part of what causes relapse into sin and addiction.

Surrender

Today I will willingly allow godly Christians to disciple me,
and I will disciple others as I grow.

Girl Power

Charm is deceptive, and beauty is fleeting;
but a woman who fears the LORD is to be praised.

PROVERBS 31:30 NIV

My LinkedIn feed once greeted me with a selfie featuring a large-breasted woman inviting haters to hate because "I'll dress how I want." Sadly, many women believe that leading with their flesh will bring recognition, and the pressure to compete fuels the lie that looking a certain way will bring fortune and fame. The media doesn't help—peddling deception through a trove of gorgeous personalities and propagating flesh and sex as the most useful tools. People jockey for influence, speak and act provocatively, and put their bodies on display. Want to know what's truly powerful? Growing into the person God created you to be. Jesus can't bless a counterfeit version of you. Your true worth comes from finding identity in him.

Surrender

Today I will remember that looks and beauty fade. I will allow God to define my worth.

Christ Is Enough

My God will meet all your needs
according to the riches of his glory in Christ Jesus.

PHILIPPIANS 4:19 NIV

More, more, more. That's the name of the game in America. Heaps of stuff are never enough. We strive for bigger houses, better jobs, more cash, the newest gadget, and the most youthful body money can buy. But it's all an empty sugar rush that runs out. If you have never told Jesus, *You are enough*, try it. You can't take any "stuff" when you leave this world anyway. Jesus died on the cross and bore the weight of sin and death for *you* to have eternal life with him. He would've done it for *only* you! What more can we possibly need? Nothing. Train your mind to focus on heaven and the things of the kingdom, and the world will quickly become an empty counterfeit that does not satisfy.

Surrender

Today I am grateful for Jesus' sacrifice, and I can truly say, "Christ is enough for me."

Kingdom Mindset

"I hold this against you:
You have forsaken the love you had at first."

REVELATION 2:4 NIV

It's easy to get sucked into the doldrums of daily living or to wake up and think it's just another ordinary Tuesday. There are seasons where life runs on autopilot with countless things competing for our attention: spouse, kids, social media, work, hobbies, and more. Many of our desires are worthwhile and honest pursuits but are dishonoring time wasters. Start dedicating the very first part of the day to the Lord before stressors build and time runs out. Yield to God before you start making plans and instead ask *him* to set your schedule. Pray that he will keep you out of things that do not glorify him or are against his will. Then go forth with resolve and peace, knowing the Lord is guiding your steps.

Surrender

Today I will remember this day is a gift and will surrender each moment to the care of God Almighty.

Don't Stop Believing

Overhearing what they said, Jesus told him,
"Don't be afraid; just believe."

MARK 5:36 NIV

People think I'm a bit crazy when I tell them God often uses secular music to give me impressions or confirmations. Back in 2012, my husband and I were walking through a deep valley. Many fearful days left me wondering if we would make it. "Don't Stop Believing" by Journey had always been a favorite song of mine, but suddenly it began playing from my radio almost every day. One Sunday, beaten down and close to giving up, I somehow managed to drag my family to church. As the worship team took their places on stage, I heard the opening chords to that same, famous Journey song I'd been encountering daily for months. Something touched my spirit: *Jesus likes Journey!* And when I believed, God was faithful to deliver.

Surrender

Today I will remember that there is power in believing the promises of the Bible.

Believing for Breakthrough

"See, I am doing a new thing!
Now it springs up; do you not perceive it?
I am making a way in the wilderness
and streams in the wasteland."

ISAIAH 43:19 NIV

Wilderness seasons can be immensely difficult, but they're also a tremendous opportunity to embrace God. A painful trial taught me this lesson. After months of struggling to make something happen, I finally surrendered and became willing to let God lead. Something absolutely transformational happened in the moment when I stopped fighting—God began to breathe new life into my situation. When I got out of the way and quit trying to control, he was able to perform a miracle in an area where I felt completely hopeless. Maybe you are waiting for something. Decide to accept God's will and watch the simple act of submission transform you.

Surrender

Today I will surrender and trust God's plan for my life.

Put Your Shame to Work

"Do not be ashamed of the testimony about our Lord
or of me his prisoner. Rather, join with me in suffering
for the gospel, by the power of God."

2 TIMOTHY 1:8 NIV

I attended my first AA meeting in 1999 after my second
DUI arrest. I remember slinking into the dingy room hoping
no one would recognize me. My position as a local news
anchor made me a "celebrity," after all. Addiction often
brings a shameful burden wrapped with lies, sexual sin, and
humiliating memories. We fear being exposed and rejected
because, underneath it all, wounds of abandonment pulsate
like abscessed teeth. Though I didn't stick around in AA for
long, God arranged some divine appointments with like-
minded people. Some had worse war stories, some not as
bad, but across the board, freedom came through sharing
secrets. Exposing past secrets to the light of day brought
acceptance and healing. Using your private shame to offer
others hope can become an incredible lifeline.

Surrender

Today I will remember that there is no condemnation for
those who are in Jesus. I will expose every secret to the light.

Go Your Own Way

"Have I not commanded you? Be strong and courageous.
Do not be afraid; do not be discouraged,
for the Lord your God will be with you wherever you go."

JOSHUA 1:9 NIV

Grandma June labeled me a "follower," always wanting
the hottest Guess jeans, Minnetonka moccasins, and other
fashions my eighth-grade classmates modeled in the 1980s.
I was a people pleaser, starving for love and validation. Two
decades of following Jesus has helped me to unlearn many
dysfunctional patterns. As our identity as a son or daughter
in God's royal family is established, he becomes the only one
worth pleasing. Superficial people and things that do not
glorify him bring strong distaste. As a foundation in Christ
continues to shore up, supreme confidence will emerge, and
the old drive to please others at the expense of yourself will
be gone for good.

Surrender

Today I will seek to please God above all else.

Power Source

*His divine power has granted to us all things that pertain to
life and godliness, through the knowledge of him who called
us to his own glory and excellence.*

2 PETER 1:3 ESV

Many addicts are extremely hardheaded. For most of
my life, despite hearing that God is an ever-present help,
God was simply a last resort for me. After I'd exhausted all
options, burned every bridge, and crashed into brick walls
a thousand times, I'd become desperate enough to offer
up a crisis prayer. My eyes were on the world around me,
convinced that it held the key to unlock my chains. Seeking
therapists, doctors, recovery meetings, and other "experts"
to help me stop drinking brought temporary change, but
nothing enduring. Real transformation happens only when
we become willing to open our hearts to Jesus. Then we can
receive the unlimited power of God's Holy Spirit to guide,
comfort, and advise us in every moment. Worldly remedies
are just a quick fix. We need something supernatural.

Surrender

Today I will pray to be filled with the Holy Spirit so I will
have the power to fight every battle.

Growth Is Imminent

From the day we heard, we have not ceased to pray for you, asking that you may be filled with the knowledge of his will in all spiritual wisdom and understanding.

COLOSSIANS 1:9 ESV

I always wished to be taller, but five feet and three inches is what God gave me. My dad used to say, "Coffee will keep you short," but since I didn't drink coffee until later in life and failed to gain more height, it must be a myth. But blocking God's way is a surefire growth killer. Instead of making things more difficult for yourself, surrender. Laying everything down for the Lord causes circumstances and perspectives to dramatically change. That's not to say you'll get everything you want or that life will become a total joyride. But God can do incredible things with a willing vessel. Putting the brakes on your own plans and seeking him will bring movement in the right direction. Things and circumstances will align. You'll feel at peace, no longer struggling or fighting to do it all alone.

Surrender

Today I will ask Jesus to remove things from my life that are stunting my growth.

Leave Things Alone

"Be still, and know that I am God.
I will be exalted among the nations,
I will be exalted in the earth!"

PSALM 46:10 ESV

Do you struggle with patience? If you do, you may feel that waiting is the hardest part of any situation. Maybe you are hopeful for something to turn around, an estranged child to reach out, or for your spouse to finally attend church. After all your efforts are exhausted, the only thing left is prayer—and waiting. It's extremely tempting to keep checking, asking, or doing something, but instead of trying to force God's timing, step back and wait. Trust that he is arranging things behind the scenes and getting situations and other people ready. Perhaps he is preparing you as well. Your breakthrough might not look exactly how you hoped it would, but you can rest assured it will be exactly what you need.

Surrender

Today I will resist the urge to meddle in things for which
I've already petitioned God.

Radical Peace

"Peace I leave with you; my peace I give to you.
Not as the world gives do I give to you.
Let not your hearts be troubled,
neither let them be afraid."

JOHN 14:27 ESV

One of the greatest gifts of a relationship with Jesus is peace that makes no sense. When the world is fretting, freaking out, and panicking, Christians can pray, surrender the issue to God, and trust that he will handle it according to his perfect will. The Bible tells us not to fear, panic, or worry and that doing so shows a lack of faith. We don't need to get spun out about the usual calamities that plague non-Christians, because we have access to an amazing God who promises to never leave or forsake us. He doesn't answer prayer according to our wishes every time, but he will always provide an abundance of supernatural peace through the Holy Spirit, who is our Comforter.

Surrender

Today I will seek the peace of Jesus through every trial and circumstance.

Unfailing Hope

The LORD takes pleasure in those who fear him,
in those who hope in his steadfast love.

PSALM 147:11 ESV

A favorite coping skill from my childhood was looking beyond my present boredom or pain to something pleasant waiting up ahead in my future. Weekends, holidays, and summer vacations brought the promise of something better. When my neighbor's dog had puppies, I begged for a new addition to the family and wrote sincere letters to my parents pledging my commitment to care for this dog. My hopes stayed sky-high until my parents finally agreed to adopt a little lab pup. Where does your hope lie today? In the world's offerings or in eternity with Jesus? The only thing worthy of true devotion is the King of kings. We sometimes get what we want in this life, but the reward that awaits us in heaven is so much more amazing than any earthly prize.

Surrender

Today I will rest in the eternal hope found in my Lord and Savior, Jesus Christ.

Change Your Mind

"If my people, who are called by my name, will humble themselves and pray and seek my face and turn from their wicked ways, then I will hear from heaven, and I will forgive their sin and will heal their land."

2 CHRONICLES 7:14 NIV

People often ask me, "After fifteen years of binge drinking and blackouts, how did you finally quit?" The answer might perplex some: I simply *decided* to. Part of repentance is the intentional act of changing one's mind and turning away from a pattern of behavior to follow a godly path. Deliverance from addiction couldn't come until I firmly decided on it. Then Providence moved! My pledge came from a deep desire to never drink again and an overwhelming sense of my rebellious life and its opposition to God. Utterly disgusted with myself, I wholeheartedly invited Jesus to take over, wash away my sin, and guide me on the narrow path that leads to him.

Surrender

Today I will ask God to reveal behaviors or sin patterns that grieve him and to help me get them out of my life.

Be Yourself

The LORD said to Samuel, "Do not consider his appearance
or his height, for I have rejected him. The LORD does not
look at the things people look at. People look at the outward
appearance, but the LORD looks at the heart."

1 SAMUEL 16:7 NIV

By nine, I already wanted to be someone else. Sitcoms and
books with fictional heroines like Nancy Drew taught me
how to look and act and what to believe. As I grew older,
the need to escape intensified, and alcohol ushered in a
Jekyll–Hyde imitation of the real me. Each time I drank, I
lost a little bit more of the natural woman God had created.
Drugs, alcohol, and other addictive drives are potent soul-
stealers, slowly chipping away at the beautiful image the
Lord intended for each of his precious children. It took
twenty years of work to reclaim my lost identity, and I found
so much freedom in embracing the authentic self my Creator
had designed. It's truly exhilarating. God won't bless a
counterfeit version of you. He wants the real thing!

Surrender

Today I repent of coveting another's life and ask God to help
me fully embrace who he created me to be.

Fate of the Wicked

God will bring every deed into judgment,
including every hidden thing,
whether it is good or evil.

ECCLESIASTES 12:14 NIV

Has someone you love ever betrayed you? If so, then you know the intense, crushing, and devastating fallout that results. Even when God brings reconciliation, total healing can take years and much pain and anguish. When a breach of trust happens, it is natural to experience lingering fear, anxiety, or doubt about whether the betrayer has truly changed. The best test of a life transformed by Jesus is consistency and truthfulness over time, along with sincere repentance and a desire to follow him. Continuous checking on someone in an effort to "catch them in the act" of some sin can be very harmful to your mental health as well as to theirs. Rest in the enormous blessing that you don't have to play private detective because God sees everything and will repay each person according to their deeds.

Surrender

Today I will cease meddling in the lives of others and will ask God to reveal to me whatever I need to see.

Release the Past

Not that I have already obtained all this, or have already arrived at my goal, but I press on to take hold of that for which Christ Jesus took hold of me.

PHILIPPIANS 3:12 NIV

Eight years into sobriety, my marriage suffered a crushing blow that seemed impossible to overcome. My husband and I exposed our sins of infidelity to each other, but instead of bringing it to the cross of Christ, we took matters into our own hands. The Lord led us through a painful eighteen-month trial before we were ready to seek intercessory prayer from Spirit-filled Christians. The Enemy would love to keep you stuck in failure, ruminating on the past and wallowing in hopelessness and defeat. Some of us drag around the sins of yesterday like a bag of stinking garbage, recycling loads of shame instead of simply crying out for forgiveness. Repentance promises a clean start through the blood of Jesus. Invite him into your mess and allow his grace to bring transformation.

Surrender

Today I will repent of the past and ask Jesus to cleanse me with his precious blood. Then I will forgive myself and move on.

Goodness Overflows

*The grace of our Lord was poured out on me abundantly,
along with the faith and love that are in Christ Jesus.*

1 TIMOTHY 1:14 NIV

Being an addict is absolutely exhausting. Addicts are
constantly in survival mode, trying to appear normal to
others while mentally planning their next binge. When I
was an active blackout binge drinker, I had little gratitude
and never even considered thanking Jesus for his constant
protection. Instead of praising him for his ever-present
help, I congratulated myself for evading police or somehow
surviving another night of near overdose. Once we embrace
a life of sobriety, we become overwhelmed with gratitude
and can't stop praising God for days of walking the earth in
service to him. We finally embrace his mind-blowing grace
and can't help but stand in awe.

Surrender

Today I will reflect upon my many blessings and thank God
for everything.

One Day at a Time

We do this by keeping our eyes on Jesus, the champion who initiates and perfects our faith. Because of the joy awaiting him, he endured the cross, disregarding its shame. Now he is seated in the place of honor beside God's throne.

HEBREWS 12:2 NLT

After Jesus delivered me from bondage to addiction, I was so on fire for him that serious hardship seemed light-years away. I expected continued blessings—simply because I was sober! Stress is much easier to manage through a clear head, but adjusting to life without chemical help isn't easy. Only years later, when I faced the toughest trial of my life, did I finally learn the true meaning of "one day at a time." The Lord can use disobedience to help us grasp our need for him, and my crisis revealed the futility of any relationship or endeavor grounded in anything other than God. We won't make great growth strides in every season of life. Sometimes clinging to Jesus like a frightened child is all we can muster. Remember that the dark times don't last forever, and a blessing awaits on the other side.

Surrender

Today I will remember that it is okay to just breathe, cling to Jesus, and ask him to show me the next right thing.

Pray First

Confess your sins to one another and pray for one another, that you may be healed. The prayer of a righteous person has great power as it is working.

JAMES 5:16 ESV

The prayers of addicts are often reactionary and crisis-oriented: *God, please don't let me get pulled over. Please don't let me get kicked out of my apartment. Please don't let the boss smell alcohol on my breath.* For born-again believers, communication with Jesus is the rock that undergirds every moment. Worshiping, thanking, and, yes, petitioning him with our requests become just like breathing. Instead of panicking when something goes wrong, we learn to saturate every decision, victory, need, and struggle with prayer. Consulting God becomes totally natural, and over time, we begin to see his faithfulness through answered petitions as well as seeing his reasons for not always granting our requests. Prayer builds our faith and provides a rock-solid foundation in a world of chaos.

Surrender

Today I will remember to pray first rather than trying to figure things out on my own.

No Frills

We may throw the dice,
but the LORD determines how they fall.

PROVERBS 16:33 NLT

Following Jesus should not be complicated, but the zeal
to become scripturally literate can be a common pitfall.
A solid biblical understanding is important, but we must
also remember the simple things. A few years ago, I began
studying different doctrinal positions and soon grew weary
of seeking assurance and an air-tight stance I could defend
and fully accept. Various scriptural interpretations seemed to
make just about any view plausible, and finding the "right"
approach remained out of reach. Then I found a teaching
about the simplicity of the gospel and the core message of
Jesus as a beautiful, no-frills offering. Spiritual growth is
essential for Christian life, but don't forget to humbly seek
God first in your quest for knowledge.

Surrender

Today I will remember to keep it simple by seeking God and
asking him to direct my path each day.

A New Heart

"I will give you a new heart, and a new spirit I will put within you. And I will remove the heart of stone from your flesh and give you a heart of flesh."

 EZEKIEL 36:26 ESV

My first public response to Jesus came at the age of nine. I'd just finished a week of Vacation Bible School, and the event capped off with an altar call invitation. My legs trembled as I followed the rest of the kids to kneel in a small circle to recite the sinner's prayer. Unfortunately, no one discipled me after my new conversion, and adolescence brought much rebellion. Even during those dark years, I know that Jesus and the Holy Spirit never left me and offered me protection from many dark forces that could have ended my life. As my downward slide progressed, the fallout of sin crushed me into submission. Surrender can be one of the hardest things, and our flesh will fight it. Be encouraged to know you don't have to struggle alone. Jesus will give you a new heart, and he will never give up on you.

Surrender

Today I give you my whole heart, Jesus. Remove the stubborn parts and replace them with willingness.

Crazy Love

You bless the righteous, O LORD;
you cover him with favor as with a shield.

PSALM 5:12 ESV

To quote a couple of old pop hits from the 1970s, I was forever "Hooked on a Feeling" or "Looking for Love in All the Wrong Places." Childhood abandonment wounds initiated an endless search for a faultless man to love. After many boyfriends, a few short-lived engagements, and one broken marriage, I was bruised, battered, and no closer to my heart's desire. After surrendering to Jesus and being delivered of addiction, my kingdom husband, Mike, came along. He truly is the love of a lifetime, but even Prince Charming arrived with baggage—just like me. After surviving a painful blow to our marriage and later being transformed by Jesus, I finally realized that no human will ever love me like God can.

Surrender

Today I will remember that Jesus loved me first and that no person will be able to love as perfectly as he does.

No Exceptions

You also were included in Christ when you heard
the message of truth, the gospel of your salvation.
When you believed, you were marked in him with a seal,
the promised Holy Spirit.

EPHESIANS 1:13 NIV

As a chubby kid, I was usually the last one picked for
every sports team. I desperately wanted to fit in but felt
awkward and uncomfortable in social situations. As a
teenager, I silenced my worsening anxiety through blackout
binge drinking, but the aftermath brought crippling shame,
escalating panic, and a worsening self-image. The kingdom
of Jesus Christ is not based on rank, class, or status. We are
all welcomed into God's family by doing a few simple things:
a desire to change, a sincere prayer of repentance, and a
belief that Jesus is who he claims to be: the truly divine and
perfectly human Son of God who died on the cross and rose
again on the third day. There are no favorites in the Lord's
family; all are invited to find new life in him.

Surrender

Today I will stop comparing myself to others and believe I
am valuable, worthy, and loved equally in God's eyes.

Love One, Love All

Whoever hates his brother is in the darkness and walks in the darkness, and does not know where he is going, because the darkness has blinded his eyes.

1 JOHN 2:11 ESV

Back when I was living in active addiction, I spent a massive portion of my mental energy focusing on a few people whom I considered to be enemies. I wanted them to "get theirs" because of how they'd hurt or embarrassed me. But the Christian life holds no place for vitriol, not even for the worst adversary. We should offer the love of Jesus to the best of our imperfect human ability, *especially* to those who prove to be very difficult to love. When we behave in harmful ways or spread hate, we burn our influence as Christians and ruin our unique witness. It isn't always easy or fair, but the Bible teaches that those who are forgiven should do the same for others. Jesus loved us first, despite our sinful human natures, and we must model his example.

Surrender

Today I will think of the person I struggle the most to love and ask Jesus to soften my heart toward them.

The Big Picture

Put false ways far from me
and graciously teach me your law!

PSALM 119:29 ESV

There's an old saying in recovery groups: "Think the use all the way through." When contemplating relapse or facing temptation, train your mind to envision the big picture of the event—the total cost. My first drinking experience brought intense euphoria and was incredibly reinforcing, creating an insatiable urge to recreate the experience. The same went for a new relationship. Every time I scored male attention, I was flooded with an intoxicating high of excitement and the feeling of being wanted. Unfortunately, I paid an extremely painful price for ignoring the package of shame, regret, and self-hatred that inevitably came with it. Sin in the form of intoxication, fornication, pride, and greed is a road to nowhere that only brings pain and destruction.

Surrender

Today I will ask Jesus to help me focus on the big picture and the consequences of my choices when I am tempted.

The Good Life

The fruit of the Spirit is love, joy, peace, forbearance, kindness, goodness, faithfulness, gentleness and self-control. Against such things there is no law.

GALATIANS 5:22–23 NIV

Back in my drinking days, my top priority was figuring out where the party would be for the coming weekend. My mind flooded with thoughts of getting drunk, listening to loud rock music, and fooling around with my boyfriend. Numbing myself with chemicals and empty affection seemed liked the good life, but I was wrong. The pursuits of lust and intoxication only brought crippling hangovers, self-hatred, and shame. Sin and wicked living stifle the fruit of the Holy Spirit—the true gifts of a godly life. Living purely and laser-focused on Jesus enables us to feast upon that which is wholesome and gives birth to growth and life.

Surrender

Today I pray for a fresh filling of the Holy Spirit—the gift that keeps on giving.

Honor the Covenant

"'The two will become one flesh.'
So they are no longer two, but one flesh."

MARK 10:8 NIV

Sharing wedding vows is one of the most beautiful and memorable experiences in life. Rarely does a couple captivated by the rapture of the moment think, *We might be on the brink of divorce a few years from now.* My wedding day to my covenant spouse, Mike, was as gorgeous and idyllic as any, yet seven years later we'd walk through an incredibly painful season. The previous year had been one of secrets and deception, as we both succumbed to temptation and broke that beautiful vow we'd made. Once the secrets were exposed, God began to work. Mark 10:8 became a lifeline, with placing our marriage on the altar our only hope. Total surrender became our saving grace. In times of indecision, fear, and turmoil, find promises from the Bible that speak to your life situation and stand upon them.

Surrender

Today I am reminded that the Word of God can breathe new
life into every situation.

Flee from Sin

Flee from sexual immorality. All other sins a person commits are outside the body, but whoever sins sexually, sins against their own body.

1 CORINTHIANS 6:18 NIV

My parents were stoic Scandinavians who avoided conflict and deep conversation, and my sex education consisted of a short lesson about the reproductive system in health class. I never dreamed of asking my mother, knowing she approached the entire topic with much awkwardness. At fifteen, I began dating an older boy and very quickly the dynamic shifted to getting physical. I didn't know sex was reserved exclusively for the marriage covenant, and one careless decision was the beginning of fifteen years of broken relationships. God yearns for us to save sexual intimacy for our covenant spouse. If you've failed in this area, don't despair. Repent of your past right away and start a new journey with Jesus.

Surrender

Today I will treat my body as a living sacrifice and will save sexual intimacy for marriage.

April

Choose Your Kingdom

Should the waters from your well flow away,
rivers of water in the streets?

PROVERBS 5:16 NLV

One day, while my husband was working toward his first reading of the entire Bible, he was deeply immersed in the book of Proverbs and remarked, "Man, there is a lot of good wisdom in here. I can only imagine all the trouble I could have avoided if I'd read it as a teenager!" The Bible boldly opposes a culture that suggests Jesus is our buddy, God is only love (and not wrath), sex can be casual, and worldly success brings happiness. Addiction overcomers know firsthand the danger in following worldly advice. We must decide which kingdom we will follow: that of this earth (sex, drugs, and rock 'n' roll) or the way of Christ Jesus (repentance, obedience, and sacrifice). Two opposing forces are vying for your soul. Which will you choose?

Surrender

Today I will choose to pursue the kingdom of God and
reject the temporary pleasures of this world.

Stay Steadfast

Because the Sovereign LORD helps me,
I will not be disgraced.
Therefore have I set my face like flint,
and I know I will not be put to shame.

ISAIAH 50:7 NIV

Having differences with our Christian brothers and sisters is healthy and normal. We might belong to different denominations, participate in radically diverse styles of worship, or gravitate toward various Bible translations. We don't have to split hairs over preferences, and generally they do not compromise our walk with the Lord. Some things are vitally important though, such as defending the deity of Jesus Christ, coming together in corporate worship, loving and serving our neighbors, sharing the gospel, and holding fast to faith in Jesus. We will gain courage and strength in knowing that, when we commit to living for the Lord and doing his will, we will never regret it.

Surrender

Today I will seek to do God's will, knowing that he will help me every step of the way.

Seeing the Light

Immediately something like scales fell from his eyes,
and he regained his sight. Then he rose and was baptized.

ACTS 9:18 ESV

Blinded to the devastating impact of addiction for years,
I was deluded into thinking my problem wasn't that bad.
Along the way, Jesus continued to bring moments of clarity
where the weight of my sin almost took my breath away.
But then the Enemy would whisper more lies, and I'd again
fall for the delusion that safe drinking was within reach.
The cycle continued for years until I finally came to the last
time I drank, August 21, 2003. The next morning, cowering
in shame and filled with misery, I desired a clean and sober
life more than anything. I repented, accepted the love and
forgiveness of Jesus, and finally stepped into the light for
good. Ask Jesus to open your spiritual eyes and to illuminate
any ways you are walking in spiritual darkness.

Surrender

Today I pray that Jesus helps me to see my circumstances,
people, and the world through his eyes.

Come Together

"I tell you that you are Peter, and on this rock I will build my church, and the gates of Hades will not overcome it."

MATTHEW 16:18 NIV

I've had many friends claim, "I'm not into organized religion. I can worship God in nature or while I'm out fishing." Others have decided not to return to church after many congregations succumbed to fear mongering and COVID-19 lockdowns. Church doesn't need to be a big fancy building. Obviously the apostles didn't gather with the faithful in cathedrals and worship halls. It's not about brick and mortar but a body of believers. Whether we're meeting in someone's home or in a large worship center, the point is praising God, receiving discipleship and correction, and enjoying fellowship. Our Creator is pleased, and there is power in gathering. Don't fall for modern conveniences that promise the same experience as regular church attendance. There is simply no substitute for the force that flows when Christians come together.

Surrender

Today I will make gathering and fellowshipping with other Christians a priority.

Demons Beware

"I have given you authority to trample on snakes and
scorpions and to overcome all the power of the enemy;
nothing will harm you."

LUKE 10:19 NIV

Too many believers have no awareness of the power
available to followers of Jesus Christ. Instead of walking
in authority, clueless people allow the devil free access to
trample them to the point of defeat. The Enemy's greatest
fear is that Christians will discover this truth and then begin
to walk in their God-given authority. Demons tremble at the
sound of Jesus' name! Stop living depressed with your head
hanging low and decide to kick the devil out for good. Break
any agreements you've made with Satan, speak the Word
over your life, put on the armor of God's Word, and decide
today that the Enemy will no longer have access to your
mind, heart, home, or family.

Surrender

Today I will take up my authority in Jesus, war with the
Word as my sword, and kick the devil out for good.

Don't Compromise

> Whoever walks in integrity walks securely,
> but whoever takes crooked paths will be found out.
>
> PROVERBS 10:9 NIV

Addiction invites a pack of lies, among them, deceptive thinking that we are getting away with something. I spent several years bartending, the perfect profession for a problem drinker. Though I started out straight as an arrow with the desire to work dutifully for my employer, after a while, having a little drink while still on duty seemed okay. One cocktail quickly became two, and before long I was sipping drinks on the job so much that I couldn't even remember driving home at the end of the night. My dirty deeds were exposed one day when the boss called me into the office and fired me. Though we might fool people for a while, sooner or later our secret life of sin will be exposed. God promises to bring every lie and falsehood to the light.

Surrender

Today I will ask Jesus to reveal any hidden areas of my life that need to be exposed.

A Family Affair

They said, "Put your trust in the Lord Jesus Christ and you and your family will be saved from the punishment of sin."

ACTS 16:31 NLV

Today's world and wicked culture can create a lot of fear for parents. We want to shield our children from ungodly examples in the public school system, the media, and their peers. Surprisingly, the most dramatic force in a child's life has not changed since the beginning of time: parents still carry the heaviest responsibility and influence over their children. Through a mother and father's witness, diligence in passing on faith, and openness to difficult conversations about sex, abortion, gender identity, and race relations, parents can push back the darkness that seeks to corrupt their children. Discipling your household and circle of influence and using your life as a living witness carries a powerful impact.

Surrender

Today I will be intentional about my witness for Jesus and the impact it has on people around me.

Best Practices

I will instruct you and teach you in the way you should go;
I will counsel you with my loving eye on you.

PSALM 32:8 NIV

Bondage to addiction throws our lives into chaos and takes us outside the will of God. When we are not abiding in him, we allow the Enemy and his demons open access to our lives, and then all hell breaks loose. At the height of my drinking, every day was a nightmare where I feared my life might implode. Maybe today would be the day my boss would discover I'd been drinking on the job, the repo man would come to the door, or my landlord would show up to demand the back rent I was forever promising and I would end up on the street. Surrendering to the will of Jesus brings peace and order because we know his plans are always good. He will never steer us wrong.

Surrender

Today I will surrender to Jesus in each moment, praying for
his perfect will to be done.

He Sees It All

The eyes of the LORD are on the righteous,
and his ears are attentive to their cry.

PSALM 34:15 NIV

Ever wonder why wicked people seem to prosper and evil agendas are allowed to flourish? We may never know during this lifetime why those who do wrong aren't brought to justice or why blatant deception stays hidden. It's especially frustrating when you've been hurt or betrayed by a friend or family member, and the offending party has not repented or made amends. Take comfort in knowing that God sees you, feels your pain, and is close to the brokenhearted. And, while it might not be obvious to human awareness, the Lord detests people who live a lie as well as those who hurt or deceive others. If they fail to seek forgiveness from him, they will pay the price for eternity.

Surrender

Today I will pray for my enemies and trust God to fight my battles.

The Way Out

"All the prophets testify about him that everyone who believes in him receives forgiveness of sins through his name."

ACTS 10:43 NIV

Prior to alcohol finding me, I was a pretty decent kid. I wasn't rebellious, I told the truth, and I obeyed my parents. But the world of addiction opened the floodgates of sin that brought increasingly negative consequences. Almost every weekend brought me to another compromising position and deep shame as soon as intoxication's deception wore off. Keeping our indiscretions hidden is hard work, and most addicts live in fear of exposure. Jesus paid a high price to cover our sin debt. We won't find freedom in temporary pleasures but only through the Savior of the world. Turn to Jesus now and receive remission for every sin.

Surrender

Today I will examine myself, ask Jesus to show me areas of unrepentant sin, and seek forgiveness.

Jesus Satisfies

Jesus declared, "I am the bread of life.
Whoever comes to me will never go hungry,
and whoever believes in me will never be thirsty."

JOHN 6:35 NIV

An old saying endures in the AA program regarding alcoholic beverages: "One is too many, and a thousand is never enough." At fifteen years old, my first opportunity of unrestricted drinking seemed to offer the secret to a happy life. Suddenly animated, self-assured, and ridiculously confident, my fear of people and their opinions had vanished. But I couldn't find a way to keep my liquid courage at a manageable level because every beer I drank just made me want more. Other partiers had off switches that allowed them to stop drinking when they had enough, but I displayed an unquenchable thirst that only passing out could silence. Alcohol and drugs are just temporary fixes that delay problems for a bit. Only Jesus can offer a lasting solution for our parched and thirsty souls.

Surrender

Today I will remember that Jesus is the only one who can truly satisfy me.

Steadfast Love

"Even to your old age and gray hairs I am he, I am he who will sustain you. I have made you and I will carry you; I will sustain you and I will rescue you."

ISAIAH 46:4 NIV

The beautiful image this verse creates always brings me to tears. How I wish I had found it sooner and believed it! For over half my life, I lived in fear of being left alone. I hated being home alone at night or watching friends drive away in their cars, and underneath it all was the feeling of rejection and abandonment—just sheer terror of aloneness. At age fifteen, I believed having a boyfriend was the answer to quiet my fears. But that first serious relationship ended when my first love moved away, leading me to countless soul-wrecking attempts to avoid my greatest fear. In 2011 while on the brink of divorce, I finally embraced the truth: Jesus was the only 100 percent trustworthy constant. Faith in him and his promise to remain with us forever can heal the deep wounds we bear.

Surrender

Today I will remember to place my trust in Jesus alone, knowing humans are flawed and imperfect creatures.

Servant's Heart

*"Let each of you look not only to his own interests,
but also to the interests of others."*

JOHN 14:1 ESV

Addiction leads a person into bondage, forcing them into a soulless shell clouded by self-absorption. The stranglehold of the substance makes it impossible to express genuine empathy for others or to attempt to lift up another during their own trials and struggles. The Big Book of Alcoholics Anonymous refers to this condition as "self-will run riot."[3] A life dominated by preoccupation with self and the burning desire to control people is exhausting and void of blessing. When we surrender to Christ, we are transformed into a new creation with a fresh desire to pour into the lives of others.

Surrender

Today I will remember that my greatest purpose is to show
the love of Jesus to others.

---

3   Bill W., Alcoholics Anonymous: The Story of How Many Thousands
    of Men and Women Have Recovered from Alcoholism (New York:
    Alcoholics Anonymous World Services, 2002), 62.

Saving Surrender

[Laban] said, "The LORD watch between you and me,
when we are out of one another's sight."

GENESIS 31:49 ESV

Experiencing a betrayal in a relationship or friendship can
seem impossible to overcome. The world offers help through
experienced therapists, medications, and best-selling books.
But there's a difference between coping and healing. Therapy
tools can help with functioning but offer little to mend the
shame, anger, and unforgiveness that accompany traumatic
events. As we scramble for quick fixes and easy solutions,
we refuse the very thing God requires—true surrender to
him. Surrender doesn't mean giving up. It is ceasing to resist
and deciding to submit to authority. It can be terrifying to
relinquish control, but the act will bring relief, freedom, and
peace. Jesus is fully able to heal every wound if only you're
willing to let him.

Surrender

Today I will believe that God knows what is best for me. I
will ask him to lead me along the perfect path for my life.

Love Rules

Faith, hope, and love abide, these three;
but the greatest of these is love.

1 CORINTHIANS 13:13 ESV

The Beatles got it right: sometimes, the one thing you really need is love. Though it sounds easy, that doesn't always stop us from overcomplicating the stressors of life by forgetting a basic fact that can save the day. Thoughtless responses often make bad situations worse, but we can avoid this by a simple attitude shift. The daughter with the messy room that stays clean a few hours and quickly returns to a state of disarray? Use gentleness, love, and maybe an offer to help her clean it. A husband who forgot something important? A tender tone, grace, and the decision to overlook a slight rather than point it out. Although we must not let the pursuit of a loving approach override the need to speak necessary truth, we can always strive to act biblically from a place of sincere devotion to the Word of God.

Surrender

Today I will commit to loving others as Jesus did, to speaking the truth from a place of kindness, and to offering grace and mercy in every situation.

Life Lessons

Keep back your servant also from presumptuous sins;
let them not have dominion over me!
Then I shall be blameless,
and innocent of great transgression.

PSALM 19:13 ESV

King David famously committed adultery with Bathsheba and then ordered her husband Uriah killed in battle. When David confessed his sins to the Lord, he was forgiven (see 2 Samuel 11–12). David deeply regretted his transgressions and begged God to help him avoid willful disobedience in the future. We must maintain a healthy perspective of our mistakes by keeping the door to the past open just a crack. This means remembering the pain and consequences of rebellion so we do not repeat them. When visiting the wreckage of days gone by, don't condemn yourself after you have sincerely repented and sought Jesus' forgiveness. After he has cleansed us, he remembers our sin no more. Just accept any correction you need, stay aware of the disastrous impact of disobedience, and don't forget the lesson you have learned.

Surrender

Today I will seek forgiveness and then release any lingering feelings of shame and self-condemnation.

Keep Your Chin Up

Whatever was written in former days was written for our instruction, that through endurance and through the encouragement of the Scriptures we might have hope.

ROMANS 15:4 ESV

My dad always used to say, "What a difference a day makes." It's remarkable how a mood or outlook on life can change so dramatically and sometimes without warning. We humans are fickle creatures. Thank God *he* never changes! Times of struggle come, and unfortunately, tough seasons might drag on far longer than we'd like. Some people must battle periods of illness, financial burdens, the untimely death of a loved one, or other calamities. Life can be hard, grief is sometimes heavy, and surviving another day becomes the primary focus. It's okay to not make gigantic strides forward. Seek Jesus and allow him to carry you through to brighter days ahead.

Surrender

Today I will remember that during life's ups and downs, I can trust that God never changes and is always there for me.

Time Management

*Plant your seed in the morning and keep busy all afternoon,
for you don't know if profit will come from one activity or
another—or maybe both.*

ECCLESIASTES 11:6 NLT

Too much free time is disastrous for an addict. Idle minds
spin a million miles an hour, seeking frivolous distractions,
and the Enemy is always at the ready with triggers,
temptations, and invitations to sin. Staying busy is vitally
important, and it is essential to intentionally focus on activities
that honor God. Beginning the day with prayer and the Bible
is not only crucial but also transformational. Make him your
priority, and he will faithfully bless the rest of your life. Serving
others, pursuing fulfilling hobbies, and taking care of ourselves
through exercise, healthy eating, and immersion in nature
are also great ways to nurture mind, body, and spirit. You will
never regret abandoning activities that do not honor God and
instead letting him guide your steps.

Surrender

Today I will seek the Lord for help with spending my
time wisely.

All Access

"If you fail to keep your word,
then you will have sinned against the LORD,
and you may be sure that your sin will find you out."

NUMBERS 32:23 NLT

I spent my years of alcohol addiction escaping danger by the skin of my teeth. I didn't want my employer to know I was hungover at work. I drove home drunk hoping to evade the police. I lied to my mother about the real reasons I needed a babysitter so I could go out drinking. Deep down, I sensed time running out like sand in an hourglass. I knew that, eventually, I would be held accountable for my lawbreaking and that it wouldn't be long before my deceptive ways were exposed. As followers of Jesus, we live with integrity because we know that sin brings great sorrow and conviction. Even if we successfully fool people, God never misses a thing. He has a way of bringing justice and correction when we're doing wrong.

Surrender

Today I will remember that I cannot hide anything from God.

Second Chances

You say, "I am allowed to do anything"—but not everything
is good for you. And even though "I am allowed to do
anything," I must not become a slave to anything.

1 CORINTHIANS 6:12 NLT

As a young person, I thought Christianity was boring
and restrictive. I couldn't imagine how hardcore church
goers experienced fun and excitement while being forced
to follow a bunch of archaic rules. I was a "C & E Christian"
(only attending church on Christmas and Easter), but I
lived like a heathen otherwise. After my confirmation in
tenth grade, I opted out of corporate worship to sow my
wild oats. Ten years later, I came crawling back, having
realized that the world offered nothing meaningful. I was
craving a community of believers, intimacy with God, and
true fellowship. The church welcomed me with open arms,
becoming the second family I didn't even know I needed.
Are you feeling lost and alone? Give church a chance.

Surrender

Today I will remember that surrendering to God and
following his rules is the pathway to freedom.

Speak Life

"Whoever desires to love life and see good days, let him keep his tongue from evil and his lips from speaking deceit."

1 PETER 3:10 ESV

Hurtful words can leave enduring scars. Often we speak carelessly and without considering the impact of our speech. So many times, I've said things I deeply regretted. Like me, you've probably been on the receiving end of harsh comments that bruised your ego and sowed seeds of pain and division. It's tempting to go off on others in the heat of the moment, to lash out in anger, or to "one up" someone with sarcasm, a sharp tongue, or a snappy comeback. Think before speaking and carefully consider your reasons. Is what you're about to share kind, necessary, or helpful? Is it true? Are you offering the comment in love? Controlling the flow of words generates life-giving power.

Surrender

Today I will pray for help with controlling my tongue. I pray I will resist the urge to speak thoughtlessly.

Fire Insurance

"The eyes of the LORD watch over those who do right,
and his ears are open to their prayers.
But the LORD turns his face against those who do evil."

1 PETER 3:12 NLT

When I was a young girl, a neighbor brought me to a local Vacation Bible School program where I was invited to recite the prayer of salvation. I didn't really understand the full implications, and discipleship did not follow my conversion. My parents dismissed my questions and the public display of faith as nothing important. Years later, I was very grateful for a sweet neighbor lady named Marge who facilitated my first authentic meeting with Jesus. But I'd soon learn that simply saying a prayer does not assure salvation. I needed heart change, along with a desire to reject sin and run toward righteousness. Reciting a prayer may be the first step, but your journey to Jesus can't end there. Pursue godliness, read the Bible, find other Christians to walk with you, and devote time to prayer. Your heavenly Father desires all of you, not just the bare minimum.

Surrender

Today I will seek God with my whole heart, listen for his voice, and obey his teachings.

Posture of Surrender

Since we know he hears us when we make our requests,
we also know that he will give us what we ask for.

1 JOHN 5:15 NLT

It's easy to forget how some of our best-laid plans started us down the highway to hell. If you've reached an impasse or a roadblock, it might be time to determine who is calling the shots—you or God? Having plans, desires, and goals is normal and, for the most part, healthy. We must make every effort to live a God-honoring life, to work, and to put our faith into action. We can't stand idly by, waiting for prayers to materialize. Sometimes we get into a pickle by praying for the wrong things or from a selfish heart space. Blinded by wants and needs, we catapult into a litany of requests without seeking God's will. Here, we find ourselves on thin ice. Before crashing through, we must stop, repent, and surrender ourselves, praying only for knowledge of his will.

Surrender

Today I repent of pursuing my own selfish desires and ask
God to take control.

Subtle Deception

Satan, who is the god of this world, has blinded the minds of those who don't believe. They are unable to see the glorious light of the Good News. They don't understand this message about the glory of Christ, who is the exact likeness of God.

2 CORINTHIANS 4:4 NLT

The devil begins his battle for our souls at birth. When I was a child, I witnessed heavy use of alcohol every weekend and at social and family functions, making drinking to excess seem normal, fun, and mysterious. It seemed to promise camaraderie and a lifted mood, which proved a powerful draw. As I entered adolescence, I remembered the mental images of those parties, and they rolled through my mind's eye like a series of colorful thumbnails. My teenage eyes were veiled from the far-reaching impact of my first drinking experience that would become the catalyst for fifteen years of blackouts. We must remain forever vigilant of the devil's quest to capture our souls by learning to hate sin as well as every false way that opposes the Lord.

Surrender

Today I pray Jesus will open my eyes to any areas where the devil has blinded me.

Ask Wisely

The Lord was pleased that Solomon had asked for this.
1 KINGS 3:10 NIV

Though my parents didn't have a lot of money, they tried to fulfill the wishes of my brother and me each Christmas. One year, I was overjoyed to receive a pair of used downhill skis with someone else's name engraved on them. As a child, the greatest joy I could think of was actually receiving the material gift I wanted for Christmas. When we are still spiritual infants, it is common to pray outside of God's will and to request material things, and our prayer life consists mainly of crisis pleas uttered in desperation. The Lord is sympathetic to our developing spirituality, but he deeply desires that we mature beyond selfish wants. Seeking wisdom from God enables us to rise above foolish, empty, and vain petitions. Wisdom is the gift that keeps on giving because it produces good judgment and discernment in all situations.

Surrender

Today, instead of seeking material things or deliverance from crisis, I will seek wisdom.

Gratitude Changes Things

Whatever you do or say, do it as a representative of the Lord Jesus, giving thanks through him to God the Father.

COLOSSIANS 3:17 NLT

Starting back when I was old enough to legally work, I was on the hunt for a get-rich-quick scheme. I recall several multi-level-marketing endeavors, telemarketing gigs that promised tons of commission payouts, and restaurant serving jobs rumored to offer big tips and high table turnovers. I was never happy in any position I held and was forever searching for the next big thing. Deep down, I knew the problem wasn't the job. It was a severe lack of identity coupled with the chaos caused by my addictive lifestyle. Perhaps you're at a place in life where things aren't going well. Maybe you hate working every day, your relationship is on the rocks, or your finances are in crisis. Start giving thanks to God for everything he has provided, even if it's not exactly ideal. You'll be amazed at how an attitude of gratitude will change your outlook.

Surrender

Today I will focus on being grateful for everything God has given me.

A Joyful Heart

Enter his gates with thanksgiving;
go into his courts with praise.
Give thanks to him and praise his name.

PSALM 100:4 NLT

Waking up hungover made me mad at the world. I even cursed the sun shining through the window blinds. We all have someone in our lives we might label a "Debbie Downer." That person is never happy and is always talking about their medical ailments, complaining about personal issues, or worrying over the latest crisis. No one enjoys being around someone like that. Finding things to complain about is easy, but cultivating a joyful outlook takes a little more effort. With intentionality and practice, it will become more natural. Start thanking God right when you wake up, even for the smallest things—water, a flushing toilet, the rising sun, food, someone to wake up to. As you pursue joy, your mood will elevate, and you'll uncover even more blessings.

Surrender

Today I will cultivate joy and focus on being thankful for
everything God has given me.

Leap of Faith

Don't worry about anything; instead, pray about everything.
Tell God what you need, and thank him for all he has done.

PHILIPPIANS 4:6 NLT

Antidepressant drugs are a multi-billion-dollar industry, and anxiety is an epidemic across the country. One look at the state of the world makes the reason obvious; so many secularists are plagued by fear that comes from idol worship and disbelief. But it is different for us. Christians are called to faith, not fear and anxiety. If we focus on the unknown, the scary possibilities, and the threats piling up daily, we will surely be gripped by terror. Many people are addicted to chaos, the news cycle, and the hit of adrenaline that comes with the next big crisis. Shifting our focus to prayer, reading the Bible, and trusting God will free us from the fear-based trap of the world. Look at your current lifestyle and take control of anything that is out of order. Praying, trusting God, and releasing your cares to him will bring peace in every storm.

Surrender

Today I will shift from focusing on my fears to building my faith in Jesus.

Firm Foundation

"If you refuse to serve the LORD, then choose today whom you will serve. Would you prefer the gods your ancestors served beyond the Euphrates? Or will it be the gods of the Amorites in whose land you now live? But as for me and my family, we will serve the LORD."

JOSHUA 24:15 NLT

Is the church really dying? Many cite dire statistics that claim our young people are leaving the faith in droves. What's the culprit? The media, public school agendas, and negative friend groups all seem likely causes. While these factors can all play roles in turning kids away from church, the most important safety net to counteract them remains the same. Godly parents. What you model to your kids has a dramatic influence on their allegiance to the Christian faith. Parents who pray together, share the Word, and disciple their children through actively practicing their beliefs have a powerful impact. While the world can feel scary and out of control, don't despair. Modeling the ways of Jesus will positively change everyone around you.

Surrender

Today I will focus on controlling what I can through modeling Christian beliefs and values in my home.

Divinely Intertwined

*"Since they are no longer two but one,
let no one split apart what God has joined together."*

MATTHEW 19:6 NLT

Marriage is a beautiful blessing designed by God to be shared between one man and one woman. Unless they are called to a life of celibacy to serve the Lord, most people are made to share their days with someone. However, a spouse should not take the place of Jesus. My search for unconditional love involved a parade of mostly well-meaning but counterfeit men, many serving as vessels for Satan and his demons. I thought having a romantic commitment (no matter how shaky) would complete me. I forced a marriage outside God's will at age twenty-one, and a couple of years later, I was the divorced single parent of a toddler. Exactly seven years after my first husband and I filed for divorce, I married my covenant spouse. Don't let feelings of loneliness cause you to make hasty decisions. Instead of trying to rush the process, pray for God to bring into your life the person he has prepared for you, and then wait on his timing.

Surrender

Today I will pray for my spouse. If I am single and searching,
I will ask God to bring my mate in his perfect timing.

May

Wisdom Works

[Jesus] added, "Pay close attention to what you hear. The closer you listen, the more understanding you will be given—and you will receive even more."

MARK 4:24 NLT

More is the operative word for addicts and the current culture alike. When I was in bondage to blackout binge drinking, every beer I drank made me crave another, and I wasn't satisfied until I passed out. In the same way, increasing wealth, racking up toys, earning titles, and seeking new adrenaline rushes is the American way. In the fourth chapter of the Gospel of Mark, Jesus teaches about various responses to his teachings and offers a different view on the idea of "more." Some people will be blind to his words and unable to respond, but those who are spiritually hungry will be desperate for what Jesus offers. Abundance means something different in the kingdom of God: Instead of pursuing *stuff*, we chase after wisdom and what God can offer. Trust and demonstrating obedience to him will reveal our priorities.

Surrender

Today I will ask Jesus for wisdom rather than material things.

Faith Moves Mountains

"What do you mean, 'If I can'?" Jesus asked.
"Anything is possible if a person believes."

MARK 9:23 NLT

Faith certainly can and does move mountains. But don't get this popular verse twisted. Belief in something doesn't mean promotion of heretical "name it and claim it" teachings that suggest we have the power to speak something into existence. Sincere faith means surrendering our will and desires to God because we trust and believe his plan for our lives. Faith means clinging to him in times of grief, sorrow, and doubt instead of letting our hearts become hard because something didn't pan out. Faith means loving, praising, and glorifying God even when our plans fail, our prayers seem to go unanswered, or we don't sense God's presence. Faith has deep roots that do not fluctuate with circumstances.

Surrender

Today I will ask Jesus to grow my faith so that I remain grounded in him even when I don't understand what he is doing.

The Great Equalizer

The godly are rescued from trouble,
and it falls on the wicked instead.

PROVERBS 11:8 NLT

Sometimes it seems like chronic sinners are getting away with something. Everyone knows a person who has not repented of evil behavior but shows no signs of distress. Perhaps they drive drunk or deal drugs, cheat people, or are not faithful to their spouse. On the outside, they are partying like rockstars and seem on top of the world. But sin carries consequences. It might not always be obvious currently, but chronic sinners cannot escape eternity. You may never get vindication, apologies, or repentance from betrayers, con artists, or abusers here on earth. But death is the great equalizer, and no one can escape it. Everyone will eventually give an account for their actions. Without Jesus, our sins will result in eternal damnation.

Surrender

Today I will repent of my sins and pray for those who are still in bondage.

Blessed Assurance

"You are blessed because you believed that the Lord would do what he said."

LUKE 1:45 NLT

I don't constantly get words or impressions from God, but sometimes he will reveal things after I've spent time devoted to prayer and diligently seeking him. A thought or idea may drop into my head later and strongly resonate—sort of like an "aha" moment. From late 2011 to early 2013, I endured a chaotic and stressful time in my marriage after my husband and I revealed to one another that we had each engaged in extramarital affairs. When I reached a breaking point, I told the Lord I wanted out of the marriage but strongly felt the directive to trust and wait. Suddenly I was filled with the peace I'd been seeking. If you're facing a difficult decision, remember that sometimes the answers don't come right away, but diligently seeking God will reveal the right direction in turbulent times.

Surrender

Today I will trust in the promises God has given me and not doubt.

Something Supernatural

Jesus called out to them, "Come, follow me,
and I will show you how to fish for people!"

MATTHEW 4:19 NLT

Lost souls are everywhere: the grocery store, the bank, the
hair salon, work, school. Begin to view each interaction
with another human being a divine appointment. Pray
for the Holy Spirit to fill you before you leave the house
in the morning or prior to going anywhere. Ask yourself,
How can I engage others? Some exchanges are brief and
passing (like a drive-thru window, checkout counter, or
when walking by someone on the street), but you can still
make an impression. Hand out gospel tracts, smile, and
greet everyone you see. Many people are distracted with
their smartphones and pay little attention; don't follow that
example. Something supernatural happens when we pray
for the Spirit to lead us. We're able to see people through the
eyes of Jesus.

Surrender

Today I will be intentional about interacting with everyone I
meet even if it's just a smile or to say hello.

Stay in Position

Humble yourselves under the mighty power of God,
and at the right time he will lift you up in honor.

1 PETER 5:6 NLT

A favorite pastor once preached a message about pride, urging his congregants to "humble yourself or let God humble you. Just know the second option will be a lot more painful." The art of humility stands contrary to a culture that promotes the pursuit of power, status, and influence. Most people want to be first, not last, to be seen, not hidden among the shadows, and to be revered, not lost in obscurity. Yet, Jesus—our ultimate role model—came to earth not to be served but to serve. The Word of God teaches that any earthly recognition we may enjoy will be short-lived. Instead, focus on glorifying God. Pleasing him will always pay off, either in this life or the one to come.

Surrender

Today I pray the Lord will teach me to be humble and to serve others rather than serving my own interests.

Show, Don't Tell

"Prove by the way you live that you have repented of your
sins and turned to God."

MATTHEW 3:8 NLT

The gospel of Jesus Christ is beautiful in its simplicity and
designed so that a young child or a person of limited intellect
can easily understand it. But reciting a prayer is just the
beginning: a willing and submitted heart will bring the fruit
of a changed life. "Don't just talk the talk; walk the walk," the
old saying goes, and this is even more important for Christ
followers. Your life can powerfully demonstrate your faith
in God and point others to eternal hope. While no one but
Jesus can live a perfect, sinless life, he is our role model.
When we fail to demonstrate love, we should be quick to
repent, ask for forgiveness, and strive to model something
different than the rest of the world. Others are watching, and
even when we fall short, grace, humility, repentance, and
genuine love will go a long way.

Surrender

Today I will ask God to help me show his love to others and
to demonstrate the love of Jesus to the world.

He Is Your Vindicator

Just before dawn the Lord looked down on the Egyptian army from the pillar of fire and cloud, and he threw their forces into total confusion.

EXODUS 14:24 NLT

Lashing out in anger or wanting to repay evil with hate is often a normal human response to being hurt, wronged, or betrayed. While living in active addiction, I moved from one chaotic circumstance to the next, forever experiencing the fallout of life lived outside God's will. With a cloud of doom always hanging overhead, I was left to con my way out of situations. Manipulating others into doing what I wanted and trying to control outcomes was exhausting. I wish I'd known back then the exhilarating freedom that comes from letting God fight for me. Instead of stressing over difficult situations you may have gotten yourself into, repent for the actions that led you there, lay all grievances and problems on the altar, and ask the Lord for help. He will faithfully demonstrate his supreme ability to fight every battle.

Surrender

Today I will ask God to fight my battles instead of taking matters into my own hands.

Eternal Reward

Lay not up for yourselves treasures upon earth, where moth and rust doth corrupt, and where thieves break through and steal: But lay up for yourselves treasures in heaven, where neither moth nor rust doth corrupt, and where thieves do not break through nor steal.

MATTHEW 6:19–20 KJV

We all like things. Stuff is nice, and possessions make us happy for a little bit. They offer distraction, bring a burst of joy to the moment, maybe even offer an illusion of superiority. Most everyone can relate to the brief hit of dopamine that comes with a new pair of shoes, a snazzy outfit, or a shiny new car. Unfortunately, like with any drug, the high quickly fades. The new clothes eventually wear out, that sweet ride develops rust spots, and the fat we paid thousands of dollars to freeze away comes back. The older we get, the more life spirals on, the fleeting nature of it laid bare. Eventually, we are forced to face the truth: it's all like fluffy cotton candy that tastes great in the moment but never truly satisfies. Instead, store up treasure by leading others to Jesus.

Surrender

Today I will focus on the only meaningful reward, making Jesus proud and awaiting eternity with him.

Help Wanted

> When Moses' father-in-law saw all that Moses was doing for
> the people, he asked, "What are you really accomplishing
> here? Why are you trying to do all this alone while everyone
> stands around you from morning till evening?"
>
> EXODUS 18:14 NLT

Trusting others and being vulnerable are difficult
endeavors. Maybe we've been burned, betrayed, or abused
and have sworn off close relationships. By age twenty-four,
I was a divorced single parent, determined to prove I could
take care of myself. Though realizing I didn't need a man
to complete me was very good, isolation eventually became
a roadblock that brought much frustration and mental
anguish. I thought I was too smart for AA, too proud for
government assistance, and too experienced to need counsel
from wise women. My greatest barrier became trusting Jesus
to bring godly people and divine appointments. The Enemy
wants us isolated and alone, but God yearns to draw us
into fellowship. We must be open to sharing life with other
Christians.

Surrender

Today I will stop trying to do life alone and instead ask God
to set up divine encounters.

Stay Salty

"You are the salt of the earth. But what good is salt if it has lost its flavor? Can you make it salty again? It will be thrown out and trampled underfoot as worthless."

MATTHEW 5:13 NLT

Some Christians are afraid to share Jesus with others because they fear being viewed as weird or pushy. As a reformed people-pleaser, I was tainted by my parents' criticism of those they disdainfully called "born-agains." But when Jesus says we (Christians) are the "salt of the earth," this is an amazing distinction. We have been called out of the world to model something other than wickedness, materialism, godlessness, and self-promotion. Our identity as Christ followers is what makes us distinctly "salty," unique from the rest of this Stepford-wife world. True Christians who follow Jesus in spirit and in truth offer rare and valuable preservation against a world that is quickly decomposing.

Surrender

Today I will ask Jesus to help me view my Christian faith as beautiful, valuable, and something I should share.

Fear the Lord

"Don't be afraid," Moses answered them,
"for God has come in this way to test you,
and so that your fear of him will keep you from sinning!"

EXODUS 20:20 NLT

Our nation has lost its healthy fear of the Lord. Many
people are pleasure-seekers, living just for today and not
caring about how their actions alienate them from a holy
God. Their sins pile up to the heavens, yet they continue to
live in wicked debauchery, promising to change sometime in
the future. Today is the day of salvation, and God is calling
you out of sin. He has been speaking to you about that secret
battle, hidden addiction, or private resentment. Near the end
of my fifteen-year nightmare spent in bondage to addiction,
I had a moment of clarity, suddenly convinced that my life
would end with a drunk driving crash, overdose, or accident.
Godly fear grew from this revelation, and keeping the door
of my past open a crack keeps me from forgetting. Having
a healthy fear of the Lord will help us avoid falling into the
Enemy's traps.

Surrender

Today I pray that my fear of the Lord will grow to help me
avoid sinning.

Holding Out

I am confident I will see the Lord's goodness
while I am here in the land of the living.

PSALM 27:13 NLT

Has God spoken a promise to your heart? Maybe months or even years have passed, and you are still waiting for a breakthrough. As the days go by, you grow increasingly weary. The eighteen months I spent fighting, warring, and battling for the restoration of my marriage were some of the darkest and bleakest I've ever encountered. But now that over a decade has passed, I see the amazing work God performed in both my husband and me during that dark time of refining. As I waited for a breakthrough and believed in Jesus for healing, I stood upon Psalm 27:13. I somehow knew I wasn't going to wait on heaven for transformation because it was going to happen here on earth. And it did! You've got to believe you're going to see God turn the situation around. He can make a way.

Surrender

Today I will ask God to breathe new life into a promise he
has spoken to my heart.

Waymaker

"I am the LORD, your Holy One, Israel's Creator and King.
I am the LORD, who opened a way through the waters,
making a dry path through the sea."

ISAIAH 43:15–16 NLT

Did you know that God loves to show up and show out?
But we can block his power when we insist on controlling
situations, people, and outcomes. At age twenty-three, I'd
been married less than two years when my then-husband
abruptly announced he was leaving. Devastated, I begged
shamelessly for him to stay, but he was resolute. After
spending six tortured days unsuccessfully pleading for him
to change his mind, I prayed for the first time in years. My
plea was not for God to override my estranged husband's
will; I just wanted peace. When morning broke the next day,
the storms within had calmed, and God had answered my
prayer. Rather than giving me what I thought I'd wanted, he
offered his peace. Does your situation look hopeless? Ask
God to breathe life your way. Then read the Bible and wait
for direction.

Surrender

Today I will ask Jesus for peace within the storm and for
knowledge of his perfect will.

Whom Will You Serve?

Humble yourselves before God. Resist the devil,
and he will flee from you.

JAMES 4:7 NLT

Ask yourself a serious question today: *Am I following the ways of the world or walking with Jesus?* Satan's goal is for us to live in isolation, self-reliance, and deception that says we can do everything alone. We don't need God; we just need money, power, influence, and followers. As I have mentioned before, the devil hooked me at a very young age, highlighting the adults nearby who drank, partied, and seemed to be having the time of their lives. He whispered, *You can experience that magic too.* The lie tasted good at first but eventually brought nothing but misery. We must resist the devil, purposely turn toward biblical truth, proclaim God's promises, and war diligently in prayer.

Surrender

Today I will make a choice to turn away from worldly
pursuits and toward God.

In His Will

The LORD directs our steps,
so why try to understand everything along the way?

PROVERBS 20:24 NLT

God is everywhere all the time. He knows every possible choice we could make as well as what we will ultimately do, and he is able to weave any action we take—including mistakes and missteps—into his grand plan. Nothing we do can thwart it. For years, I struggled to intellectualize where I stood regarding soteriology, the doctrine of salvation. Am I a Calvinist, Arminian, Provisionist, or something else? Does it even matter? As I continue to flesh this out, I believe God has some divine decrees that nothing can move, but he also offers free will outside of the non-negotiables. However you slice the free will debate, surrender is the way to go. A self-run life brings nothing but disaster, so seek the center of God's will.

Surrender

Today I will pray for Jesus to help me surrender my will to his sovereign plan for my life.

Justice Is Served

Don't let them say, "Look, we got what we wanted!
Now we will eat him alive!"

PSALM 35:25 NLT

Have you ever prayed for an enemy to be put to shame?
I certainly have, and that's what King David appears to be
doing in the verse above. While living a life of drug use and
wickedness, we naturally become exposed to some unsavory
characters. Sadly, some of these people will not be happy for
us when we escape the jaws of addiction. Some may even
hope for our demise or wish for our speedy return to the
evils of substance abuse. It may be tempting to want our
accusers to meet disaster, but we should avoid taking matters
into our own hands. We need to pray for our enemies, trust
God to protect us, and allow him to fight our battles.

Surrender

Today I will pray for my enemies to turn from sin and find
Jesus. I will trust God to fight my battles.

Fulfilled Dreams

Hope deferred makes the heart sick,
but a dream fulfilled is a tree of life.

PROVERBS 13:12 NLT

Through many years of failing to find freedom from addiction, I never lost hope. Inside, a tiny flame of promise was pointing the way out of the darkness. But sometimes when hope is deferred, the temptation to move things along can be overpowering. Trying to force God's hand pushes us outside the boundaries of his perfect will. My first marriage was a prime example: instead of waiting for the man God had chosen, I manipulated a situation and paid the price. Whenever we find ourselves trying to influence our situations for our own gain, we're in dangerous territory. Instead, decide to trust God, and don't allow pride and control to take over. Make the right choice.

Surrender

Today I pray that Jesus will help me to be patient and that I will trust him as I wait.

Paying the Piper

"They have planted the wind and will harvest the whirlwind.
The stalks of grain wither and produce nothing to eat.
And even if there is any grain, foreigners will eat it."

HOSEA 8:7 NLT

This verse is dramatic, powerful, and just a little foreboding.
So what exactly did Hosea mean? God was warning Israel
that planting something worthless would reap a harvest
of negative consequences, which it did in 722 BC when
Assyria invaded the country. I spent fifteen years worshiping
the idol of alcohol, and being trapped in blackout binge
drinking caused a boatload of negative consequences. The
tornado took years to manifest, but what seemed fun in
the beginning brought the desecration of my body, loss of
purity, divorce, financial ruin, legal problems, and emotional
consequences. The first step toward freedom was true
repentance and a desire to turn from the idol I had placed
before the Lord. Do you have gods that are replacing God?
Repent today.

Surrender

Today I will ask God to reveal any idols I have put before
him. I will repent and turn from sin.

Total Trust

"Remember the things I have done in the past.
For I alone am God! I am God, and there is none like me."

ISAIAH 46:9 NLT

God controls the flow of everything. Nothing is random, and we can safely gather from Scripture that God either *causes* things to happen or *allows* them to. He is omniscient, knowing every thought we will think and every action we will take. But he doesn't *control* all of that. Say I want to buy a Chevy Camaro. I go to the website and build the car I want, exerting my free will in the process, but before I order it, I prayerfully consider what God's will would be. His voice is clear to me because I have saturated everything with prayer. My time in prayer brings me to the conclusion that despite my desires, the choice that would please God most here is to put all of that money toward something else. While God would not stop me from charging ahead and buying the car anyway, I choose to listen to his voice instead. This is what it's like walking in God's will. We saturate everything with prayer, surrender to him, and simply trust.

Surrender

Today I will remember to saturate everything I do with prayer and remain obedient to God.

All Have Fallen

Everyone has sinned; we all fall short of
God's glorious standard.

ROMANS 3:23 NLT

Think of the person who has hurt you the most. Maybe it's a bully from high school, a coworker, that person who tried to steal your spouse, or even your own parent. Now imagine that person as a little infant made in the image of God. Jesus loves your enemies, wants their souls to be saved, and has commanded us to forgive even those who aren't sorry or don't deserve it. Let's face it—if we're honest, we know we don't deserve forgiveness either. We have all sinned and fallen short of God's glorious standard. Loving and praying for your enemies is not easy, but it is a biblical mandate, and it frees us from bitterness and resentment.

Surrender

Today I will ask God to show me anyone I am struggling with, and I will ask him to help me to forgive.

Book of Love

You saw me before I was born.
Every day of my life was recorded in your book.
Every moment was laid out before a single day had passed.

PSALM 139:16 NLT

Psalm 139 speaks some of the most beautiful words in the entire Bible. We learn of the Father's great love for us and his amazing attention to detail while receiving a small taste of the intimacy he wants to share. God's love transcends the love of earthly fathers, cherished lovers, and any other human being. We are fearfully and wonderfully made, designed to do good works for the Father. Knowing we serve an almighty God who takes such incredible care over every aspect of our lives brings great comfort. Nothing we do takes him by surprise, and we can rejoice in knowing his eyes never leave us. Fear disappears when we place our trust in the one who wrote the book of our lives.

Surrender

Today I will thank God for caring about every aspect of my life, down to the smallest detail.

Unstoppable God

The LORD has made everything for his own purposes,
even the wicked for a day of disaster.

PROVERBS 16:4 NLT

Genesis chapter three details the sin of Adam and Eve and man's fall from grace. Many people choose to live outside God's will, but this doesn't thwart his divine decrees from being accomplished. Sometimes we experience suffering we didn't cause, like an illness without a reason or innocently being caught in the path of someone else's rebellious actions. But we also cause pain with our own decisions to do what we know is wrong. God still uses problems, evil, and adversity for the good. When you've sinned or messed up, repent and allow God to transcend your mistake. He is always in control, his mercy never fails, and his plans are always best.

Surrender

Today I will trust God even when his plans don't make sense.

True Change

"Remember not the former things, nor consider the things of old. Behold, I am doing a new thing; now it springs forth, do you not perceive it? I will make a way in the wilderness and rivers in the desert."

ISAIAH 43:18–19 ESV

Following Jesus changes everything. When we repent, believe, and accept him as our Lord and Savior, we are freed from sin, shame, and regret. After my deliverance from alcohol addiction in 2003, I vowed I was finally done drinking. But just a week later, I received a strange call from a man I had met the last time I drank, and he invited me to a beer bash. I agreed to attend despite my better judgment, but the date fell flat when my new friend realized I wasn't going to drink or party. Despite the unexpected temptation, I stood firm in my commitment to sobriety. Doing the right thing brings something very refreshing each day—a clear conscience and freedom from guilt.

Surrender

Today I will remember that rebuilding trust with others takes time.

No Guarantees

Why, you do not even know what will happen tomorrow. What is your life? You are a mist that appears for a little while and then vanishes.

JAMES 4:14 NIV

My husband is a master planner. He creates dinner menus for the week and outlines an entire calendar of events and activities months ahead of time. He also did a phenomenal job of ensuring that we would have a nest egg for the next chapter of our married life. Being responsible and anticipating future needs and challenges is important, but many people tend to make elaborate plans without first consulting God. Our lives are fragile and come without any guarantee, and Jesus wants us to remain constantly aware of our need for him. Tomorrow truly is a mystery in his hands, so we must approach each day with an attitude of surrender and willingness. Start each morning trusting God to arrange all the pieces.

Surrender

Today I will remain open to God's leading and surrender to his plans for the day.

Addicted to Love

[Love] always protects, always trusts,
always hopes, always perseveres.

1 CORINTHIANS 13:7 NIV

From age fourteen, my childhood abandonment wound drove an intense addiction to the wrong kind of love. I was searching for someone who would never leave, and my desperation brought attention from the wrong people. Instead of praying and waiting for God to send my kingdom spouse, I pursued bad boys, rebels, and people who were interested in my body but not my mind. It wasn't until much later in life when I met the one who adores me like no one else—Jesus! Human love is great, but the unconditional intimacy of the heavenly Father is the only devotion that will never fail.

Surrender

Today I will rest in the arms of Jesus, who loves me with perfection.

Safe Haven

"For a brief moment I abandoned you,
but with deep compassion I will bring you back."

ISAIAH 54:7 NIV

Refusing to obey God's will brings a boatload of pain and disappointment. At twenty-one, after ignoring numerous red flags, I married someone Jesus had not chosen for me. Moving six hundred miles south of my hometown didn't help matters, and soon I was begging to go home. Jumping to countless external reboots did nothing to help my crumbling relationship. A couple of short years later, I was a divorced single parent, lost and completely unhealed. Instead of addressing the true root of an addiction, many people seek quick fixes like moving to a different city, changing jobs, or seeking a new relationship. The change of scenery might help temporarily, but it won't address the true problem—we have rebelled against the will of God.

Surrender

Today I will be quick to repent when I disobey God.

Think like Him

"Who has known the mind of the Lord
so as to instruct him?" But we have the mind of Christ.

1 CORINTHIANS 2:16 NIV

When I was living in active addiction, my thinking was totally polluted. I was self-absorbed, fearful of others exposing my secret life, and surrounded by people who had no interest in God. Expressing compassion for others is impossible when we are deeply ensnared by our own problems. A relationship with Jesus Christ brings the power of the Holy Spirit and a brand-new mind, enabling us to think like him. When we have repented of addiction, we are finally able to move out of selfishness and step into service. We are still flawed humans until the day we die, but as we grow in relationship with Christ, we become more like him every day. Our primary purpose becomes giving, serving, and pointing others to Jesus.

Surrender

Today I will pray for the mind of Jesus and the ability to see others like he does.

Change Is Possible

"Everything is possible for one who believes."
Immediately the boy's father exclaimed, "I do believe;
help me overcome my unbelief!"

MARK 9:23–24 NIV

Overcoming addiction can be tough—if not impossible—without the assistance of our powerful God. Before long, it starts to feel like nothing will ever change. Maybe you've tried, failed, and relapsed so many times that you've given up. We all struggle with lack of faith and unbelief, and sometimes believing in ourselves is the hardest task of all. But no human weakness surprises God. Rather than being ashamed of our failures, we can seek a firm foundation with roots deeply anchored in the truth of Jesus. Instead of looking at manmade odds and past mistakes, turn to God. Never underestimate the sheer power of belief in his authority and what he came to accomplish. Building identity in him and his promises is the key that makes all things possible.

Surrender

Today I will ask Jesus to grow my faith and help me overcome unbelief.

First Response

Rejoice always, pray continually, give thanks in all circumstances; for this is God's will for you in Christ Jesus.

1 THESSALONIANS 5:16–18 NIV

I've spent much of my life trying to "figure out" God's will. Well, here it is! Rejoice, pray constantly, and be thankful. Praise him in and for all things. Sincere gratitude is miraculous. It is truly the key to opening all of life's doors. Gratitude unlocks hard hearts, makes forgiveness freely flow, and cultivates a mindset that finds blessing and abundance in every moment, no matter the circumstance. The Bible says that God inhabits the praises of his people. Simply beginning to worship Jesus by stepping into his presence will transform an apathetic or downcast heart. Start singing praises to the Lord, thanking him, and meditating on his majesty. You'll be amazed at the difference these actions will make in your heart, mind, and attitude.

Surrender

Today I will thank Jesus for everything and ask him to transform my heart and mind through gratitude and worship.

Rock Steady

Consequently, faith comes from hearing the message,
and the message is heard through the word about Christ.

ROMANS 10:17 NIV

For most of my life, I paid little attention to the Bible. I had the vague sense that I was *supposed* to read it, but I didn't take action until I was well into my twenties. How I wish I'd known the incredible power right at my fingertips! We waste a lot of time devouring social media posts, scanning internet articles, and analyzing comment threads, captivated by these choice little morsels of gossip. Most of the conversations do next to nothing to build our faith. Instead of feasting on trash, get into the Word of God. The Bible is truly transformational, and the God-breathed pages literally change us from the inside out. Reading out loud is especially powerful because the spoken Word provides armor against the attacks of the Enemy and the pressures of life.

Surrender

Today I will pray for the desire and dedication to read the
Bible every day.

June

Know Your Worth

We know that our old self was crucified with him so that the body ruled by sin might be done away with, that we should no longer be slaves to sin.

ROMANS 6:6 NIV

I spent years trying to gain approval from human beings, quickly becoming a master at changing personas to accommodate people. Underneath it all was an insatiable desire to be loved and accepted. By compromising myself in hopes of avoiding rejection, I gave up little pieces of my soul, and deep down I didn't think anyone would want me. In exchange for my willingness to betray myself, I received temporary companionship but no appreciation for my true self. Jesus offers freedom from the desire to please people. His love is perfect and unconditional. Genuine followers seek to walk in his ways and to grow more like him, and his deepest desire is that we come to know our great worth in him.

Surrender

Today I will cease trying to please others and seek only the approval of my heavenly Father.

Faith Builders

Consider it pure joy, my brothers and sisters, whenever you face trials of many kinds, because you know that the testing of your faith produces perseverance.

JAMES 1:2–3 NIV

I ran into an old friend one day, and we caught up on each other's lives. "Life is good. The family is doing great!" he beamed. Every single one of us relishes the glowing moments when our world is populated with happy, healthy kids, abundance, and prosperity. But the joyful times never last forever. The Bible tells us that the sun shines on both the just and the unjust, and sometimes bad things happen to good people. Our earthly journey is punctuated by death, disappointment, job loss, accidents, and other consequences of living in a fallen world. Instead of dreading the inevitable setbacks, use them as faith builders. The longer you walk with the Lord, the more convinced you will become of his constant presence and faithfulness.

Surrender

Today I will thank God for his constant presence when I am going through difficult times.

Purge Fear

The Spirit God gave us does not make us timid,
but gives us power, love and self-discipline.

2 TIMOTHY 1:7 NIV

An addictive lifestyle is incredibly fear-based. When we pollute ourselves with drugs and alcohol, we allow the devil and his demons free footholds and open passes to both our mind and body. Idolizing mood-altering chemicals creates an abundance of terror. We're afraid of exposure, failure, the judgment of other people, abandonment, even the thought of living without chemicals inspires dread. As the situation spirals, fear becomes the root for other strongholds. But fright responses do not come from God—it's a tool used by the Enemy to keep us in bondage. We must rebuke all demonic spirits in the name of Jesus and seal all entry points with the blood of Christ. Sometimes prayer from others is needed to help break agreements with fear, renounce associated spirits, and pray for the Holy Spirit to bring healing.

Surrender

Today I will pray for help in dealing with unresolved fears.

Life Renewed

"I have been crucified with Christ and I no longer live,
but Christ lives in me. The life I now live in the body,
I live by faith in the Son of God, who loved me
and gave himself for me."

GALATIANS 2:20 NIV

When I was little, I aspired to someday join the Army or become a competitive swimmer. At twelve, my dream shifted to being an astronaut. But by the time I hit fifteen, I'd quit thinking about college plans and began searching for keg parties. No one comes into the world aspiring to be an addict or alcoholic, myself included. But the gaping hole inside that had not secured meaning in Jesus found temporary relief in cheap beer, casual flings, and empty promises. When we become willing to break addictions and seek healing in Jesus, everything changes. Our life of sin and death is redeemed by his blood, and we become brand new creations.

Surrender

Today I will ask Jesus to make me a new creation through
the power of his finished work on the cross.

Trust in Him

"Do not let your hearts be troubled.
You believe in God; believe also in me."

JOHN 14:1 NIV

As a clueless baby Christian twenty years ago, I shared from the fourteenth chapter of John at my father's funeral. I didn't know what I was doing, but I figured John's Gospel was the place to look for scriptural wisdom. Back then, I was still addicted and six relapses away from redemption, simply searching for a good, old-fashioned funeral verse. Any newcomers to the Bible will find a compelling introduction to Jesus in John's writings. The seven "I am" statements, the numerous miracles he performed, and a detailed account of his deity make it clear that he is God, and in that, we find the ultimate assurance. Jesus' words just prior to facing his own death can bring us comfort in every circumstance. He knew the way then, and he still reveals it today.

Surrender

Today I will have confidence and courage in hard times,
knowing Jesus is with me.

Come One, Come All

God so loved the world that he gave his
one and only Son, that whoever believes in him
shall not perish but have eternal life.

JOHN 3:16 NIV

I remember feeling so proud when I finished summer
Vacation Bible School. I had successfully memorized the
names of all sixty-six books of the Bible as well as the most
famous verse, John 3:16. I figured my parents would be so
impressed by my dedication. Though I could parrot the well-
known Scripture verse, my understanding of Jesus' sacrifice
was limited. I couldn't articulate much more than, "God sent
his Son to die on a cross for our sins," but that was enough.
After receiving a fresh filling of the Holy Spirit years later,
John 3:16 took on a new meaning. It's still one of my favorite
Bible passages, especially the part that says *everyone* who
believes in him is welcome at the heavenly party.

Surrender

Today I will remember that the message of salvation is
simple. All it takes to follow Jesus is to believe in him,
confess who he is, and repent.

Comeback Kid

The LORD blessed the latter part of Job's life more than the former part. He had fourteen thousand sheep, six thousand camels, a thousand yoke of oxen and a thousand donkeys.

JOB 42:12 NIV

Everyone loves a good sequel or comeback, and there's something special about seeing an underdog prevail. To call Job an "underdog" is an enormous understatement. Despite being an upright and blameless man who diligently followed God, Job suffered extreme adversity through no fault of his own. It's truly a difficult thing to see good people forced to walk through undeserved and unspeakable pain. Job spent a long time crying out to God, wrestling with questions and confusion, and suffering, but his faith didn't waver. In the end, he was richly rewarded for his steadfastness. We can all learn a little something from this devout man from the oldest book of the Bible.

Surrender

Today I will pray for help to stay strong and to trust Jesus when life is hard.

Holy Roller

He brought out Israel, laden with silver and gold,
and from among their tribes no one faltered.

PSALM 105:37 NIV

The Holy Spirit is not an energy force, an electrical feeling, or a paranormal visitor. He has distinct personhood, and he is God. Surrender enables the activation of the Spirit and an increased sense of divine presence. After experiencing marriage restoration, my husband and I were set on fire for Jesus. One Sunday, an African evangelist spoke at church. After the service, we approached the man of God for prayer. As he grasped our hands, the presence of the Holy Spirit became so strong that we both started shaking violently. "Close the door on the past and never speak of it again," the evangelist urged, then prophetically spoke Psalm 105:37 over us. Invite the Holy Spirit to be your personal guide. You'll experience the best ride of your life.

Surrender

Today I will pray for the Holy Spirit to fill me and to lead me into all truth.

Simon Says

Do not merely listen to the word,
and so deceive yourselves. Do what it says.

JAMES 1:22 NIV

Many people think they are going to heaven simply because they said the sinner's prayer as a kid. I believed the same thing. At a young age, I invited Jesus into my heart, but discipleship did not follow my conversion, and by the time I was fifteen, I had descended into sin and rebellion. The Bible tells us we cannot just *say* we believe in Jesus, but we must also demonstrate our conversion through the fruit of a changed life. If we truly love Jesus, we will keep his commandments. We must model Christian living in faith, word, and deeds, along with daily repentance. True disciples of Christ help their neighbors, pray for others, and are passionate about leading lost people to the light of the Lord.

Surrender

Today I will pray for help to obey Jesus and to keep his commandments.

Somebody's Knockin'

Submit yourselves, then, to God.
Resist the devil, and he will flee from you.

JAMES 4:7 NIV

Dealing with the devil can be a delicate dance. We cannot ignore his existence; neither should we become overly fixated on him. A healthy vigilance about the Enemy of our souls is important to mount a proper defense. The devil attacks through the battleground of the mind and by activating people around us. Keeping tabs on thought patterns is vital because the adversary loves to assault our thinking with fiery darts that come through condemning thoughts, shame, or discouragement. Pay attention to daily interactions with others. If you're feeling activated or upset by someone, consider that spiritual warfare may be the culprit. Pray for discernment of possible spirits and refuse to let the Enemy take control of your emotions.

Surrender

Today I will ask Jesus to open my eyes to the devil's schemes so I can ask for help to resist them.

Upside Down

Humble yourselves before the Lord,
and he will lift you up.

JAMES 4:10 NIV

Addicts are often impulsive creatures who are notoriously terrible about delaying gratification and who seek drugs and alcohol to change unpleasant emotional states rather than processing problems in healthy ways. In recovery, we must learn to work for a reward and to put in effort knowing the payoff will come later. Life is like this for believers—a great prize is waiting, but first we must toil away on earth. We follow the ways of Jesus, put ourselves last, live humbly, and serve others. But sacrifice now will become joy later, and Jesus promises that he will elevate us for our obedience.

Surrender

Today I will focus on serving others and living like Jesus did.

Life on Loan

LORD, I know that people's lives are not their own;
it is not for them to direct their steps.

JEREMIAH 10:23 NIV

Most of us know someone who died way too young. Maybe they were diagnosed with an incurable disease or became the victim of a fatal accident. While it's devastating and impossible to understand why babies pass away in their sleep, healthy people get sick and die, or freak accidents happen, God is our Creator and gets to decide how many days on earth we will have and when we will take our last breath. Our lives are truly "on loan." This doesn't mean we should act foolishly, test the Lord, or fail to take precautions. But instead of living in fear, we can trust that earth is temporary and focus on our permanent residence in heaven with Jesus. Make the most of every day and truly live as though today could be your last.

Surrender

Today I will pray for God to help me to trust, surrender, and obey the promptings of the Holy Spirit.

Top Priority

Set your minds on things above,
not on earthly things.
COLOSSIANS 3:2 NIV

Life comes with many stressors and worries. *How will I pay the bills? Will my kids turn out all right? What if I stay single forever? Is this diagnosis going to be the end of me?* Too often we are trapped in the whirlwind, paralyzed by unknowns, and struggling to just hold it all together. When our circumstances are the focal point, we are rendered powerless, but shifting the attention to Jesus changes everything. Take a moment to step back from whatever challenge is holding you captive. Pray for God to come in and begin to influence the situation. Bring the matter to him and surrender it, trusting in his ability to handle the outcome.

Surrender

Today I will seek God first and trust him to control every aspect of my life, down to the smallest detail.

True Service

"Not everyone who says to me, 'Lord, Lord,' will enter the kingdom of heaven, but only the one who does the will of my Father who is in heaven."

MATTHEW 7:21 NIV

This Bible passage can paralyze even the most devout Christian with an overpowering feeling of dread. While Jesus does not want us to live in fear of whether we'll make it into eternity, he also doesn't want us deceived. The Jewish leaders of Jesus' time—the Pharisees—were hypocrites who performed good deeds in an effort to earn public honor and respect, not because their hearts were filled with love for people. The will of the Father is pretty simple: to love God, to advance the kingdom, and to love and serve others. Truly loving people means living from a sacrificial heart that desires to please the Father in heaven, not to gain the praise of men. If we love the Lord, we will also honor him by walking in his ways and pursuing holiness.

Surrender

Today I will pray for God to give me a desire to love him purely and to serve others with a sincere heart.

Lay It Down

"Come to me, all you who are weary and burdened,
and I will give you rest."

MATTHEW 11:28 NIV

Life is exhausting for a practicing addict or alcoholic.
Carrying the heavy burden of sin, lies, and shame takes
a massive toll until the weight of all that extra baggage
starts to feel inescapable. I used to start most days with a
crippling hangover, overpowering nausea, and a body weak
from abuse. Trying to hide my habits from others required
unbelievable energy, and feeling joy or excitement was next
to impossible. Jesus is waiting to lift the overwhelming
burdens you're trying to manage in your own power. I know
it might seem hard to believe, but just try it. Imagine placing
all your troubles, sins, worries, addictions, and fears at Jesus'
feet. You will be amazed by the amount of relief you will
experience.

Surrender

Today I will lay all my burdens at the foot of the cross and
ask Jesus to carry them.

Your Will Alone

> Going a little farther, he fell with his face to the ground and prayed, "My Father, if it is possible, may this cup be taken from me. Yet not as I will, but as you will."
>
> MATTHEW 26:39 NIV

Have it your way," the old Burger King slogan urged. Getting what we want when we want it is the American way. The overriding message of our culture screams big dreams, stretch goals, financial windfalls, and lifetimes of luxury. Very few motivational gurus or self-help coaches ever suggest seeking guidance from God. Some of the biggest mistakes I've made in life were due to forcing my own agenda. Even when I knew I was making a bad choice, I stubbornly refused to ask God to show me the right way. We can avoid so much disappointment, frustration, fear, and regret when we simply submit our plans to the Lord. Saturate every prayer you deliver to Jesus with the desire for his will to be done.

Surrender

Today I repent of trying to do things alone and will fully submit to God's will.

Endless Love

Those who know your name trust in you,
for you, LORD, have never forsaken those who seek you.

PSALM 9:10 NIV

Every human has a deep desire to be truly known and still loved despite their shortcomings. My father had a lot of flaws. Yet his love for me was deep. Contemplating Dad's imperfections offered perspective on my heavenly Father's devotion. Vast, limitless, and perfect, Following God means realizing that he *knows* you. Not just on a surface level but deeply, intimately, and incomprehensibly. Many people are driven by emotions and lose faith when they can't sense or feel God's presence. It's time to go beyond feeling to believing. God is always with you whether you're aware of him or not. When faith sags, dive into the Word, pray, and seek other strong Christians to help.

Surrender

Today I will earnestly seek the Lord and trust his love even when I can't feel it.

Call on Him

"Call on me in the day of trouble;
I will deliver you, and you will honor me."

PSALM 50:15 NIV

I had a very powerful nightmare several months ago. In the dream, I was out running on a deserted scenic highway, and I suddenly found myself on the ground with two men pointing guns in my face. *I somehow knew this would happen one day*, I thought, blindsided by panic. Instinctively, I began to pray in my heavenly language under my breath, so terrified that sound barely escaped. Suddenly one guy dropped his gun and demanded, "What is she saying?" My strength returned, and I began praying very loudly and shouting, "Jesus! Jesus!" The men jumped into their truck and drove away. While this was just a dream, it carried one great truth. There is power in his name, and those with faith to believe it can rest assured he is only a call away.

Surrender

Today I will pray for Jesus to grow my faith. I will remember the power in Jesus' name and will call on him in times of trouble.

Don't Hold Back

Dear brothers and sisters, I plead with you to give your bodies to God because of all he has done for you. Let them be a living and holy sacrifice—the kind he will find acceptable. This is truly the way to worship him.

ROMANS 12:1 NLT

Did you know that completely surrendering all of yourself to Jesus is an act of worship? He doesn't just want the shiny pieces or the areas you've tuned up. He desires everything. All that shame you're holding on to? Bring it to the foot of the cross, repent, and let him wash you clean. Those embarrassing stories you cringe to recall? Give them to Jesus. How about the pride and vanity you hide away in your heart? We can't conceal a thing, and trying to offer God only the good stuff creates a relationship block. Get honest with God about the things you're hiding and the areas in which you struggle. Ask him to help you gain victory over your shortcomings. Simply say, "Here I am, Lord. Use all of me for your glory."

Surrender

Today I will give myself to Jesus and hold nothing back. I will trust him to make something beautiful from my life.

Let Him Lead

We live by believing and not by seeing.

2 CORINTHIANS 5:7 NLT

Alcohol addiction made me a spoiled child. It was my way or the highway, and I continued to invite situations God had not intended and then melted down when they fell apart. Once the inevitable happened with whatever man I was pursuing, I was left deserted and miserable. Through many failed relationships, broken engagements, and one painful divorce, I ignored red flags to pacify my deep need to avoid abandonment. Jesus had a kingdom husband up ahead, but instead of waiting on him, I took detours that brought damage and pain. If only I had submitted to God! His plans for our life are so much greater than anything we can design for ourselves.

Surrender

Today I will ask Jesus to direct my steps, and I will obey the promptings of the Holy Spirit.

High on Health

Don't you realize that your body is the temple of the Holy
Spirit, who lives in you and was given to you by God? You do
not belong to yourself, for God bought you with a high price.
So you must honor God with your body.

1 CORINTHIANS 6:19–20 NLT

Living in active addiction trashes the mind, body, and soul.
Addicts are on a suicide mission, in nightmare self-destruct
mode, and hell-bent on taking ourselves to death's door.
Polluting my body with massive amounts of alcohol made
a healthy lifestyle impossible. I made half-hearted attempts
to change, started exercise programs, committed to diets,
and disciplined myself to "cut back," but everything failed
while alcohol was part of my life. Blinding hangovers made
exercise and healthy eating impossible, and I spent every
day trying to survive. The first order of business in your
new journey to health is cutting out chemical poisons. Then
receiving God's love and respecting yourself will follow.
Proper nourishment, intentional movement, and spiritual
food found in the Bible can miraculously transform the body
we once abused.

Surrender

Today I will stop abusing my body and commit to treating
myself as God intended.

The Way to Life

"The LORD our God said to us in Horeb,
'You have stayed long enough at this mountain.'"

DEUTERONOMY 1:6 ESV

My blackout binge drinking spanned fifteen long years. Like most substance abusers, I rejected the truth. Rather than bringing enjoyment, each drinking experience caused intense shame and self-hatred. Sometimes I faked control with short sobriety breaks, but they never lasted. Countless mornings of hangovers, massive withdrawal sickness, and agony over the stupid things I'd done trapped me in a self-imposed prison. My final dead end came on that dreadful day of drinking in August of 2003. The following morning, I begged Jesus to deliver me, and he was faithful to answer my desperate cry. Have you been battling an addiction or addictive behavior for years without success? Jesus wants to set you free.

Surrender

Today I will ask Jesus to reveal patterns that keep me stuck and to help me find true freedom by walking in his ways.

Good Company

Blessed is the man who walks not
in the counsel of the wicked,
nor stands in the way of sinners,
nor sits in the seat of scoffers.

PSALM 1:1 ESV

It's a story older than dirt: as a teenager, I fell in with the wrong crowd. My associates weren't bad people—just lost ones looking for belonging much like me. One day during freshman year, my eyes settled on a young man in the very last seat of the school bus, and suddenly I was captivated. He became the catalyst for many firsts: my first serious relationship, my first sexual experience, and my introduction to unrestricted drinking. My parents didn't investigate my extracurricular activities, and very quickly, I was on the highway to hell. As my alcohol abuse intensified, I found people walking the same path, and so I justified higher levels of sin. God had also placed kind, honest, and devout people along the way, but my eyes had become blinded to them. Choose your company wisely.

Surrender

Today I pray for Jesus to open my eyes to recognize people, places, and things that corrupt my character.

Eyes on the Prize

Do not be afraid of sudden terror
or of the ruin of the wicked, when it comes.

PROVERBS 3:25 ESV

Just watching the news these days can be more than
enough to depress a clown. So many people have refused
the light of Jesus as guidance through the dark world and
instead live under demonic deception. The Bible offers
stark warnings of pending disasters that could occur in our
lifetime—calamities, conflicts, rumors of wars, and the rise
of the antichrist—but we cannot know their specific timing,
and we shouldn't dwell on harbingers of them. When we
have the protection of Jesus that comes from a life submitted
to his lordship, we will walk in complete freedom, knowing
that even death cannot snatch us from his hand.

Surrender

Today I will keep my eyes from worldly and negative
circumstances and stay close to Jesus.

Shelter from the Storm

"I form light and create darkness;
I make well-being and create calamity;
I am the LORD, who does all these things."

ISAIAH 45:7 ESV

Many people are deluded into thinking that sobriety will ensure a lifetime of smooth living. While it's definitely easier approaching problems and challenges with a clear head, disappointments, unanswered prayers, and even trauma and grief will still happen. Refusing to accept the storms of life can create resentment, bitterness, and self-pity when the tornado eventually tears through. Praising God when the waters are calm is easy, but the true mark of a surrendered life is our response to unexpected trials. In times of strife, remember that nothing lasts forever, and trust in God's sovereignty. With his help, we will take comfort in knowing that everything is temporary and find total peace in his presence.

Surrender

Today I will trust God to walk with me through every season of life.

Uphold the Law

> "If it does evil in my sight, not listening to my voice, then I will relent of the good that I had intended to do to it."
>
> JEREMIAH 18:10 ESV

Whether we are simple peasants or influential leaders, every sinful act carries a consequence. When our wicked living and disobedience seem to go unnoticed, it can make us think we are getting away with something, only to have it explode in our faces. The Lord detests sin, particularly the sins of leaders, pastors, and other authority figures whom he has placed in positions of role models. His Word also commands that we submit to elected officials in positions of authority but only when they're behaving according to God's Word. We shouldn't condone decisions leaders make that are in direct opposition to biblical teachings. Pray for rulers to come into alignment with the Bible, to be convicted of wrongdoing, and to lead the people in accordance with the will of God. He will surely judge those leaders who fail to uphold his laws.

Surrender

Today I pray for people in positions of authority. I ask the Lord to help them lead biblically.

Reject Pride

"When his heart was lifted up and his spirit was hardened so
that he dealt proudly, he was brought down from his kingly
throne, and his glory was taken from him."

DANIEL 5:20 ESV

Many have dedicated their lives to achieving attention and
admiration. We measure worth through social media likes,
shares, and followers. Are we on fire for Jesus, or are we
more interested in glorifying ourselves? Every day we see the
fallout from love of self; the lives of famous church leaders,
politicians, and celebrities implode because of scandal. The
Lord detests pride more than just about anything. Jesus
Christ is God in the flesh, but he meekly washed the feet
of sinners. Instead of galloping in with all the pomp and
circumstance deserving of royalty, he humbly rode on a
donkey. He could've spared himself the agony of the cross,
but he embraced it instead to save humanity. He is pleased
when we strive to model him, to think of others before
ourselves, and to take a servant's role. If we submit to his
authority, in due time, we will be exalted.

Surrender

Today I pray the Lord will strip my pride and help me to be
humble.

Don't Fight It

"We all fell down, and I heard a voice saying to me in Aramaic, 'Saul, Saul, why are you persecuting me? It is useless for you to fight against my will.'"

ACTS 26:14 NLT

I live in Minnesota, which means that a measurable amount of snow remains on the ground for at least four months each year. Instead of shelving the running routine that keeps me sane during the bleak winter months, I strap on my Yaktrax, a type of traction cleats, and hit the highway. Though I'm grateful for the ability to stay active in the cold, wearing these contraptions feels a whole lot like running in quicksand. It reminds me of how it is to fight God's plan. Everything we try to accomplish without his involvement or blessing will become an uphill battle. Though it might seem to work for a time, running the race without God will eventually become a dead end. Instead of fearing his plans, rest in the assurance that he knows exactly what is best.

Surrender

Today I ask Jesus to open up the path that leads to his perfect will and to free me from anything that isn't his idea.

Let Loose

Let no one pass judgment on you in questions
of food and drink, or with regard to a festival
or a new moon or a Sabbath.

COLOSSIANS 2:16 ESV

When I first started walking with God, I was overly zealous
and got upset if I didn't act perfectly. If I missed a day of
Bible reading or let a curse word slip out, I condemned
myself. Unfortunately, we all know that seemingly righteous
believers who follow the "rules" of Christianity can
sometimes live a life of evil in secret. Looking devout does
not equal a repentant heart cleansed of sin, and good works
and striving don't make us right with God. We are saved only
through faith in Jesus and his finished work on the cross.
When we are made new in Christ, we are no longer bound
by stringent religious requirements. Unrestricted by the law,
we can walk in complete freedom.

Surrender

Today I will cast off religious rules and put my faith and
trust in the finished work of Jesus.

Faith in Action

Jesus immediately reached out his hand
and took hold of him, saying to him,
"O you of little faith, why did you doubt?"

MATTHEW 14:31 ESV

Do you really believe Jesus is who he claims to be? If you
do, then it's time to start living like it. So many of us walk
around defeated, hopeless, and worried about the future.
We act as though we are not truly heirs to his throne. Get
your mind right and believe the promises of the Bible. The
Scriptures are loaded with references about the power of faith
as well as how Jesus rewards those who put action behind
a deep desire. If you are waiting for a promise you know
the Lord has spoken to you, pray for confirmation and then
start acting like it is on the way. Put your faith to work and
demonstrate your devotion to God with the way you live.

Surrender

Today I will ask Jesus to grow my faith and help me to
believe his promises.

July

True Colors

"Woe to you, scribes and Pharisees, hypocrites! For you are like whitewashed tombs, which outwardly appear beautiful, but within are full of dead people's bones and all uncleanness. So you also outwardly appear righteous to others, but within you are full of hypocrisy and lawlessness."

MATTHEW 23:27–28 ESV

A scan through a typical social media feed reveals a treasure trove of fakery. Most everyone is showing the world only what they want it to see. Vacation photos of happy couples, families smiling around dinner tables, and teenagers posing with wholesome grins beam back from almost every page. But so many shiny faces are hiding private battles, secrets sins, and ruined lives. Every single person is dealing with something, and being honest about our own battles can bring hope and healing to others. Without struggle, where is the testimony to inspire others? There is much power in authenticity and willingness to get real. Remove the mask and show who you really are, and you'll be amazed by the outpouring of support you'll receive. You'll help others too!

Surrender

Today I will stop trying to impress people by presenting a fake existence. I will be who I am and allow God to inspire others through me.

Looks Can Be Deceiving

The LORD said to Samuel, "Do not look on his appearance or on the height of his stature, because I have rejected him. For the LORD sees not as man sees: man looks on the outward appearance, but the LORD looks on the heart."

1 SAMUEL 16:7 ESV

In our beauty-obsessed culture, we face constant pressure to be gorgeous, to never show signs of aging, and to appear twenty-five years old at fifty. Despite all the emphasis on exteriors, true radiance is an inside job. As we grow with the Lord, a yearning for wisdom replaces the drive for attractiveness, the desire to be filled with the Holy Spirit outweighs the carnal drive for a perfect body, and the need for peaceful moments with God overrides the drive for adrenaline and excitement. As time passes, we realize our human frames are just earthly tents dying a little more each day and the soul is what needs the most attention. Our most pressing desire becomes saving people and bringing them with us into heaven.

Surrender

Today I will ask Jesus to renew my mind, body, and soul. I will remember that beauty comes from a quiet spirit and reverence for the Lord.

True Repentance

Peter said to them, "Repent and be baptized every one of you in the name of Jesus Christ for the forgiveness of your sins, and you will receive the gift of the Holy Spirit."

ACTS 2:38 ESV

Though the gospel at its core is simple, being a true disciple of Jesus Christ requires more than just reciting a little prayer. Like many youngsters, I knelt at an altar with other kids and asked Jesus to come into my heart. I maybe even said, "I'm sorry for my sins." But a few short years later, I was a habitual binge drinker and fornicator. What went wrong? Unfortunately, millions of people have a religious experience like mine, where discipleship does not follow. Unless repentance also happens, the Bible says we are doomed. Without repentance, we are not truly saved. Salvation follows repentance, and striving for godliness *should* follow salvation. If that doesn't happen, it's likely that real repentance and salvation never occurred in the first place. True heart restoration means having genuine sorrow for how we have lived and a desire to turn from sin to pursue the teachings of Jesus.

Surrender

Today I will ask Jesus to change my heart and help me follow his example.

Sin Corrupts

"If you do well, will you not be accepted?
And if you do not do well, sin is crouching at the door.
Its desire is contrary to you, but you must rule over it."

GENESIS 4:7 ESV

At fifteen, Guns N' Roses was my favorite band. Their music screamed to me every waking hour, and I was a walking billboard for the band by wearing their garish t-shirts. Today, I can stomach only a rare few heavy metal tunes from the 1980s. Hearing such music reminds me of my sinful youth. True conversion should result in sincere disgust about our former lifestyles. Those who cussed like sailors, slept around without a care, or listened to music with filthy lyrics will find these behaviors extremely abhorrent when they find Christ. They will want to avoid environments like dark bars or places where sin and worldly entertainment are on display and the Holy Spirit is being stifled. If our heart has truly changed, we will detest everything that opposes God and strive to honor him by avoiding sin.

Surrender

Today I will sincerely repent of anything I have done
to grieve God and ask him to help me avoid future
disobedience.

Burn Brightly

It is you who light my lamp;
the LORD my God lightens my darkness.

PSALM 18:28 ESV

We do all sorts of embarrassing and shameful things as addicts, so why do we worry about how people will judge us when they learn we are Christians? When I became filled with the Holy Spirit in 2013, I kept it quiet. For a long time, I obsessed about people's reactions to my newfound faith. I feared the judgment of others more than I wanted to serve God and worried about impressing others instead of broadcasting my belief in Christ. But over time the burden of hiding such a wonderful secret became too great to bear. Eventually, I began to step from the shadows as an unashamed, born-again, Spirit-filled Christian. Resist the urge to shrink back, play it safe, and conform to the world. Wear your faith loudly and proudly. Your identity as a follower of Jesus is the most important thing about you.

Surrender

Today I will ask Jesus to help me to be bold and courageous in sharing my Christian faith.

The True Way

Simon Peter answered him, "Lord, to whom shall we go?
You have the words of eternal life."

JOHN 6:68 ESV

After experiencing life as a follower of Jesus, we come
to the realization that only he can bring the fulfillment
we crave. Though I grew up in church, I fell away for ten
years after being swept into addiction, people-pleasing,
and pursuit of the New Age movement. Although I never
completely rejected Jesus, I enjoyed shocking peers and
adults alike by dabbling in witchcraft, fortune telling, and
spell casting. Everything I explored was a dead end, and I
felt such emptiness from every alternative to the God of my
youth. Like the Prodigal Son, I finally returned to my roots.
Every counterfeit offering just pointed back to Jesus, the one
true God.

Surrender

Today I will stop searching the world over for answers, and I
will turn to Jesus, the one who has everything I need.

Next Level Faith

For to me to live is Christ,
and to die is gain.
PHILIPPIANS 1:21 ESV

Don't misunderstand me, it is sad when someone passes away. Still, it's mind boggling how the world descends into epic mourning for people who live to be one hundred years old. After all, who would really want to live forever? Many people are terrified of dying and do everything within their power to avoid it. Anti-aging treatments are a multi-billion-dollar industry, and finding the fountain of youth is an endless quest. But we will all face a final appointment. Because of his rock-solid faith, the apostle Paul welcomed death. He wanted to see Jesus face-to-face so badly that he couldn't decide which was better: spending more time on earth to win souls or dying to be with Christ. May we remember that eternity with the Lord is an out-of-this-world reward.

Surrender

Today I will pray for an eternal mindset that allows me to see beyond temporary circumstances.

Tables Turned

"Abraham said, 'Child, remember that you in your lifetime received your good things, and Lazarus in like manner bad things; but now he is comforted here, and you are in anguish.'"

LUKE 16:25 ESV

Jesus teaches through the book of Luke the sad story of a man who enjoyed every earthly pleasure but rejected God and ended up in hell. During my addicted years, I often thought I was getting away with something, and for brief periods of time, it seemed true. I'd show up for work hungover and unprepared but somehow escape the boss's notice. I'd recklessly spend my rent money, and my landlord would grant me an extension. Or I would drive home from the bar drunk and evade police. But my "luck" ran out when the Lord allowed crushing consequences to push me to repentance. Even when we think we are getting away with something, God sees all. We will eventually have to account for everything we do.

Surrender

Today I will make choices realizing that God sees everything, and I will ask him to help me do things that honor him.

Who Are You?

Jesus said to them, "Truly, truly, I say to you,
before Abraham was, I am."

JOHN 8:58 ESV

Imagine that someone proposes the common introductory prompt: "Tell me a little bit about yourself." How would you answer? Most of us will respond by diving into demographics, titles, or roles: "Well, I live in Toronto. I am married to so-and-so. I have six kids and a thriving vegetable garden." These identities upon which we place so much importance will eventually fade away. A life with enduring meaning only comes with belonging to God's family as a beloved son or daughter. Above all, we should embrace our identity as Christ followers and ambassadors for him before putting stock in any earthly title. Everything else is just a temporary assignment that dies with our earthly bodies.

Surrender

Today I will ask Jesus to show me my true value as his
precious son or daughter.

Part Ways

Jesus said to him, "Do not stop him,
for the one who is not against you is for you."

LUKE 9:50 ESV

My first serious attempt to get sober was in 1999. I'd been arrested for drunk driving for the second time that year and knew my situation was dire. Needing to do something drastic, I called up my closest drinking buddy as soon as I bonded out of the holding cell. "I'm going to quit alcohol and try AA meetings," I declared. I will never forget the long pause or the words that followed, "Are you sure you really *need* that?" You might feel completely alone after deciding to abandon your addiction while your fellow party pals seem to escape the problems addiction brings, but if you are truly serious about change, you must cut ties with dissenters. The reward you'll earn for obeying God's leading is priceless and could save your very life.

Surrender

Today I will pray for the strength to sever relationships with people who don't support me and ask God to send new Christian friends.

Share Your Story

"Go therefore and make disciples of all nations, baptizing them in the name of the Father and of the Son and of the Holy Spirit."

MATTHEW 28:19 ESV

The command to lead others to Jesus didn't stop with the early church. It remains a call to action for every Christian. While the thought of professing faith in Christ can make many people uncomfortable, sharing the miraculous things God has done in your life will build bridges like nothing else. Most people are interested in hearing a personal testimony, and it's hard to argue with a witness shared straight from the heart. Forcing belief in God is not necessary, but we can't stay silent about his awesomeness either. Faithfully share your story, and the Holy Spirit will do the rest.

Surrender

Today I will share my personal testimony with someone and let the Holy Spirit work.

Total Restoration

"Whom heaven must receive until the time for restoring all the things about which God spoke by the mouth of his holy prophets long ago."

ACTS 3:21 ESV

Years spent in addiction seem like wasted time. Looking back, I cringe at squandered opportunities, broken relationships, and days spent wallowing in shame and regret. My own father started drinking innocently at eighteen, and by fifty-four, he was in hospice care with a failing liver. Over the years, family and medical professionals alike begged him to quit, but he refused. As addiction progresses, change becomes increasingly difficult, and soon we may convince ourselves that it's too late. Whether you are a teenager or an elderly person, there's still time to turn to God. Commit to following him and ask him to free you of addictions and strongholds. You will be amazed at how he can make up for lost time.

Surrender

Today I will surrender anything I have been holding back from God and trust him to restore the years I have wasted in addiction and living outside his will.

Please God

Am I now seeking the approval of man, or of God?
Or am I trying to please man?
If I were still trying to please man,
I would not be a servant of Christ.

GALATIANS 1:10 ESV

I so envied the young ladies who performed on the hockey cheerleading squad at Proctor High School. They were the cream of the perfect crop, but on Friday nights, even the goody-goodies sometimes crashed a gravel pit party to sip a few beers. One night, a popular girl befriended me in her drunken state, and I gladly shared my wine coolers and Marlboro Lights, thinking we might become true friends. Back in uniform on Monday, she passed me in the hallway with a look of scorn. During high school and into adult life, I hungered for the approval of people and did not prioritize God. Relying on humans for praise will bleed your very soul of its life force. Strive to please God and no one else.

Surrender

Today I will repent of the times I've tried to win the approval of man. I will strive to please only the Lord.

Remain in Him

"I am the vine; you are the branches. Whoever abides in me and I in him, he it is that bears much fruit, for apart from me you can do nothing."

JOHN 15:5 ESV

Surrendering an addiction can be terrifying. Most of us have used our vice to cope, to numb fears, and to avoid pain. The very thought of losing the tool we think helps us function can be positively panic inducing. We cannot even fathom life without it. How will we have fun? Or socialize? I used to believe that living without alcohol would be dull, depressing, and meaningless. Being around people who were enjoying drinks after I'd given up alcohol made me feel like an alien. But when I asked God for help and truly wanted to change, the Holy Spirit transformed my mindset. Ask him to help you desire a new start. Putting Jesus at the center of everything and relying on him for strength to face each day will be the best decision you've ever made.

Surrender

Today I will remember that I can do nothing without Jesus. Putting him at the center of my life enables me to do all things.

God Loves It When You Sing

Sing to the LORD, bless his name;
tell of his salvation from day to day.

PSALM 96:2 ESV

Music can change your mood like nothing else. As a kid, hearing a good song would instantly put me in a positive mindset. Lyrics about sin and debauchery drew me like magnets when I hit adolescence, and I was blissfully unaware of the impact of the music infiltrating my soul. As a born-again Christian, I am not a puritan about music, and I don't listen to hymns 24/7. But the Holy Spirit brings discernment and conviction when lyrics, songs, and musical performances are in opposition to the teachings of Jesus. Being aware of what we are agreeing with while singing or being entertained by music is paramount. I am free to enjoy everything from gospel to '80s rock ballads as long as I obey the Holy Spirit.

Surrender

Today I will pay attention to the words and sounds I allow into my ear. I will ask the Holy Spirit to provide guidance.

Subject to Change

You do not know what tomorrow will bring.
What is your life? For you are a mist that appears
for a little time and then vanishes.

JAMES 4:14 ESV

How can any human grasp the frailty of life? Most people anticipate having so much time ahead that contemplating death feels morbid and unnecessary. Future plans fill our calendars like life will go on forever. But even if we're blessed with a long, full, human existence, it's unlikely we'll live beyond one hundred years. Eternity, on the other hand, is infinite. Start thinking beyond this temporal earth and pursue kingdom goals, like winning souls for Jesus and serving others like he did. There is nothing more worthwhile than revealing God to others. When making plans, seek God's will first. We are his vessels serving him on this earthly ride.

Surrender

Today I will pray for God's will to be done in all areas, and I will remain flexible to his leading.

Supernatural Security

He has made everything beautiful in its time.
He has also set eternity in the human heart;
yet no one can fathom what God has done
from beginning to end.

ECCLESIASTES 3:11 NIV

Many psychologists believe that dying is a human being's greatest fear. Facing the unknown, being alone, and feeling uncertain about what happens after life ends all play a role in our attitude about death. The Bible teaches that these feelings are actually normal because God has written on the human heart the desire to be immortal. With faith in Jesus, we can be assured of a seamless transition from this life to the next, just like stepping into an adjacent room. He created our soul—our mind, will, and emotions—to live forever. Reserving a place with Jesus Christ in heaven through repentance and belief in him is our most important assignment in this earthly life.

Surrender

Today I will remember that my soul lives eternally. I will thank God for preparing a home for me in heaven where death does not exist.

Resurrection Power

"You will receive power when the Holy Spirit has come upon you, and you will be my witnesses in Jerusalem and in all Judea and Samaria, and to the end of the earth."

ACTS 1:8 ESV

Growing up in a traditional Presbyterian church, I did not hear much discussion about the Holy Spirit. My parents, God bless them, advised me to stay away from the "crazy" people who claimed to speak in tongues. At twenty-six, I discovered the power of the Holy Spirit to teach, comfort, guide, and direct. Over the next several years, I was led to water immersion baptism as well as intercessory prayer to receive spiritual gifts. With the Advocate's guidance, we can face every challenge. The very presence of God within us will meet every need and serves to convict, comfort, and empower us to follow Jesus. Pray for a greater filling of the Holy Spirit today.

Surrender

Today I will pray for the Holy Spirit to fill me with his power, guidance, and wisdom.

Set Free

*"I say to you, Love your enemies
and pray for those who persecute you."*

MATTHEW 5:44 ESV

Experiencing a changed heart is a truly incredible experience. After suffering a blow to my marriage, I harbored a ton of bitterness toward the others involved. As time went by, God convicted me of my superior attitude and revealed that I was as big a sinner as anyone. Forgiveness took years, and genuinely wishing for my enemies to be blessed took even longer. The first step was willingness. Though it may feel impossible, Jesus commanded us to not only forgive but to also pray for our enemies. It is a very tall order to accomplish alone, but God will pour out abundant grace in the process. Forgiveness brings freedom from the heavy yoke of hatred, offense, and vengeance, bringing peace and serenity along with it.

Surrender

Today I will remember that harboring unforgiveness keeps me in bondage.

Life Everlasting

Jesus said to her, "I am the resurrection and the life.
Whoever believes in me, though he die, yet shall he live."

JOHN 11:25 ESV

A few years ago, I attended a very sad and unexpected funeral. My best childhood friend had lost her healthy and exuberant life partner at age fifty-one to a massive cardiac arrest, leaving her understandably stunned and devastated. The man who had just died was a strong Christian, which provided sincere comfort. At the service, the pastor read the well-known story of Lazarus' resurrection from the grave. "None of us thought we would be here just a month ago," he said. "I want to ask you, where are *you* with Jesus?" Then the minister pushed things a bit further: "If you were to die today, would you go to heaven?" Make sure you know your future home, and don't be afraid to ask the people you love about theirs. Eternity is at stake.

Surrender

Today I will take comfort in knowing that giving my life to
Jesus means spending eternity with him when I die.

Redeemed

To grant to those who mourn in Zion—to give them a beautiful headdress instead of ashes, the oil of gladness instead of mourning, the garment of praise instead of a faint spirit; that they may be called oaks of righteousness, the planting of the LORD, that he may be glorified.

ISAIAH 61:3 ESV

Fifty years of living has included some missteps. I wish I hadn't lost my virginity at fifteen, given myself away to people who didn't love me, or forced a marriage outside God's will. But God has an amazing way of using human mistakes and disobedience to bring glory to his name. For example, my beautiful oldest daughter would not be here had I not married her father. I can also use the regrets produced by teenage me to teach my own daughters about the priceless gift of saving sexual intimacy for marriage. Take your sin, missteps, and regrets and lay them at the feet of Jesus. He will turn them into blessings you never imagined.

Surrender

Today I will stop feeling ashamed of past choices and instead submit them to God to use for good.

Change of Heart

"Repent therefore, and turn back,
that your sins may be blotted out."

ACTS 3:19 ESV

I tried to stop drinking many times between 1999 and 2003, with periods of sobriety lasting as long as eighteen months. Though I found peace in swearing off alcohol, I'd inevitably pick it up again. My final year of binge drinking was marked by six devastating relapses, each episode creating unimaginable shame and regret. I desperately wanted to know the secret. *What would ever be different? How will I stop for good?* The problem was that my best efforts were temporary. One morning, many years into addiction, I came out of a horrifying blackout in a strange motel room and uttered a desperate cry: *Please God, don't let me drink again.* This became the most important prayer of my life. Become committed to the changes you desire and pray for God's help, and he will do the rest.

Surrender

Today I will stop trying to change in my own power. I will seek God's help and trust that he can accomplish what seems impossible.

Keys for Life

The true light, which gives light to everyone,
was coming into the world.

JOHN 1:9 ESV

Early recovery can be exhilarating. We're doing a brand-new thing, our minds are clear, and we see the world through fresh, unpolluted eyes. Some self-help circles refer to it as "the pink cloud syndrome," the feeling of giddiness that comes in the first stages of sobriety, and recovery experts actually caution newly sober folks to beware of it. While in this state of mind, we feel super charged and on top of the world and can't imagine anything disrupting our bliss. The first eight years of sobriety were this way for me, but eventually I learned that I couldn't live off the high of the "pink cloud" the way I had been. It couldn't sustain me or bring me joy; only Jesus could. When my cloud of giddiness was disrupted by a marriage crisis, I realized that my husband and I were doomed without the trifecta that saves all: repentance, forgiveness, and surrender. Jesus is the answer to all of life's problems.

Surrender

Today I will stay grounded by starting each day with
repentance, forgiveness, and surrender to Jesus.

Turn to God

> "If you return to the LORD, your brothers and your children will find compassion with their captors and return to this land. For the LORD your God is gracious and merciful and will not turn away his face from you, if you return to him."

2 CHRONICLES 30:9 ESV

Sin is just as addictive as drugs and alcohol, and relapse can be a frustrating side effect of both. You might miss the old life for a while, but as the Holy Spirit begins his transforming work, you'll begin to change. Seeking God's face and deciding to live for him will begin to realign your desires. You will still make mistakes, but as your sanctification process progresses, you will soon hate what displeases God and earnestly desire his will. Your wants and goals will look different as God molds them to his. When you make mistakes or sin, it's okay. Just be quick to recognize it and seek forgiveness. Jesus will never rebuke you for asking.

Surrender

Today I will thank God for the work he is doing in my life and ask him to strengthen my desire to follow him.

Today's Gift

The Lord is not slow to fulfill his promise as some count slowness, but is patient toward you, not wishing that any should perish, but that all should reach repentance.

2 PETER 3:9 ESV

I've known many who have lost their battles with addiction. Some were close, like my father, an old boyfriend, and even my best drinking buddy. Others were acquaintances from high school or people I had met on social media. Quite a few were treatment center clients. Many had stories very much like mine—they did reckless things, drove drunk, and got so high that they overdosed. Some never woke up or were victims of fatal car crashes. Almost all thought they had a lot more time left and that one more relapse wouldn't hurt. Every choice to drink or use is a risk that can end in death. Today, let us thank God for his protection and abundant grace. May we not abuse his goodness by testing him.

Surrender

Today I will thank God for protecting me from so many bad choices. I will treat my life like a precious gift and use it to help others.

Clear Conscience

From that time Jesus began to preach, saying,
"Repent, for the kingdom of heaven is at hand."
MATTHEW 4:17 ESV

Much of the gospel is agreeable and easy to swallow. Believe in Jesus, accept him as your Savior, and prepare for a sweet ride all the way to heaven, right? Not so fast. What about the sin stuff? Jesus presented belief and repentance as a package deal. Making a commitment to honor him as Lord and Savior comes with a mandate to follow his ways, not just to recite a little prayer. Repentance should flow naturally from a changed heart. Some churches only preach love and grace, but let's not forget the rest of the story. God is love, but he is also holy. Hell is real, eternity is at stake, and we must sincerely grieve about the way we have dishonored God and desire to change our ways.

Surrender

Today I will ask Jesus to reveal areas of unrepentant sin. I will seek forgiveness and move on with a clear conscience.

Set in Stone

Draw near to God, and he will draw near to you.
Cleanse your hands, you sinners,
and purify your hearts, you double-minded.

JAMES 4:8 ESV

I spent four years trapped in a back-and-forth tug-of-war to stop drinking. After being scared straight by my second drunk driving arrest in one year, I white-knuckled through eighteen months of sobriety before convincing myself social drinking was safe. Accepting the reality that I would never have control over alcohol use was unfathomable, so I swung wildly between two desires of wanting to remain sober and wanting to keep alcohol in my life. My pointless efforts to manage the demon of addiction just compounded the pain and shame. Until we release the delusion of control, nothing will change. Decide you've had your share of misery and ask God to remove the obsession to drink or use drugs. When you sincerely seek him, he will meet you with his grace.

Surrender

Today I will pray for Jesus to help me walk in obedience.

Walk the Talk

> Be doers of the word,
> and not hearers only,
> deceiving yourselves.
>
> JAMES 1:22 ESV

The book of James famously admonishes us that "faith by itself, if it does not have works, is dead" (v. 17). We can't simply profess to be Christians who love others but refuse to serve people. We can't walk past a suffering person and just look the other way. Claiming to love people means we stop talking badly about them and quit displaying hatred toward others. The old song says, "They will know we are Christians by our love," but many non-believers accuse followers of Jesus of being anything but loving. Faith in action means helping people, sharing what we have, dying to self, and giving our time, money, and talents. Then we are not just talk but are true disciples of Christ.

Surrender

Today I will put my faith into action by giving my time to someone.

True Devotion

"If you love me, you will keep my commandments."

JOHN 14:15 ESV

Many people who consider themselves Christians are completely deceived, and it isn't surprising. Though I never totally rejected my childhood faith, for decades I didn't understand what following Jesus really meant because no one discipled me. As a teen, I dabbled in New Age practices, jokingly referred to myself as a witch, drank excessively, and fornicated. Never once was I concerned about possibly going to hell for my wickedness. After quitting drinking in 2003 I repented of much, but I still pursued my own agendas with no clue about how I was grieving God. In 2013, I was filled with the Holy Spirit and experienced the love of the Father in a completely new way. As we grow in the Holy Spirit, old selfish desires will begin to disappear, and we will truly wish to model the ways of Jesus.

Surrender

Today I will seek the will of Jesus in everything I do and pray for him to show me the path forward.

Driver's Seat

He said to all, "If anyone would come after me, let him deny
himself and take up his cross daily and follow me."

LUKE 9:23 ESV

I used to think taking up my cross meant doing something
difficult, bearing a burden, or suffering in some other way.
I see things differently now. My biggest struggle as a Christ
follower has been learning the art of surrender. Attempts
to control and manipulate outcomes have blocked the true
freedom of a fully submitted life. I'm still a work in progress,
but amazing grace has flowed since I gave all my burdens
to Jesus. My radical deliverance from alcohol addiction,
the transformation of my marriage, and the freedom I
found when I left a job that had become unbearable—each
situation represented a time when I finally let Jesus take
the wheel. Decide today to put God in the driver's seat
completely, and you'll experience miraculous results.

Surrender

Today I will surrender to Jesus whatever burdens I am
carrying and trust his will to be done.

Paid in Full

He said to the woman,
"Your faith has saved you; go in peace."

LUKE 7:50 ESV

Born-again virgins are becoming a popular trend these days, with people who were once sexually active committing to a life of chastity until marriage. Many of us failed to keep ourselves pure, so if you can relate, don't despair. Addictions often come packaged with a lot of sexual sin, and being compromised by drugs and alcohol can lead to sinful behavior that having a sound mind would have prevented. My years spent under the spell of drinking brought much regret and shame, and I lived in constant fear of people exposing me. No matter what you have done, Jesus can completely redeem the past and offer a fresh start. Repent and recommit your body and life to Jesus today, and he will wash you clean.

Surrender

Today I will lay my past mistakes at the foot of the cross and ask Jesus to cover my sins with his precious blood.

August

Be Ready

"Behold, I am coming soon.
Blessed is the one who keeps the
words of the prophecy of this book."

REVELATION 22:7 ESV

The last chapter of the book of Revelation concludes with a stunning promise: Jesus is coming soon! Since then, people have analyzed current events and prophesied the end drawing near. Today, we see increasing natural disasters, pandemics, rumors of wars, and extreme divisiveness. Are the last days upon us? What does that really mean? Some expect a rapture of Christians before or during the tribulation while others contend the Lord will return to establish his earthly kingdom without a spontaneous disappearing act. No matter your view on end times teachings, we should all agree on living as though today could be our last. Make sure you are right with God, tell people how much you love them, and be ready to meet Jesus.

Surrender

Today I will make sure I am right with God and with the people I love.

Reimagine Prayer

You, beloved, building yourselves up in your most holy faith and praying in the Holy Spirit.

JUDE 1:20 ESV

Unlike many others, I wasn't familiar with the television evangelists of 1980s except that we as a family did *not* watch them. Because of this, the gifts of the Holy Spirit were elusive until I was twenty-six, and unfortunately, my first introduction beamed me right back to the days of questionable healings and telethons about sowing seeds with big donations. No, thank you, I wanted none of that! But the Lord in his goodness kept foreshadowing the power available through the third person of the Trinity—the Holy Spirit. In 2013, I received prayer and, shortly afterward, a heavenly language. I am now able to intercede in perfect alignment with God's own will. Coming into his presence has completely transformed me. Pray for a fresh filling of the Holy Spirit and his gifts. You'll bring your Christian experience to the next level.

Surrender

Today I will ask someone to pray over me for the gifts of the Holy Spirit.

True Followers

"Beloved, do not imitate evil but imitate good.
Whoever does good is from God;
whoever does evil has not seen God."

3 JOHN 1:11 ESV

We are saved by grace through faith in Jesus Christ. This is a rock-solid and enduring promise. But knowing this truth doesn't mean we can go on living like godless sinners, ignoring the abundant Scriptures that teach repentance, the reality of hell, or the importance of being born again. True acceptance in Jesus Christ as Lord and Savior requires a posture of surrender that will bring a total transformation. Real followers of Christ develop a strong distaste for sin, a desire to save and serve other people, and an intrinsic drive to follow the commandments of Jesus. Our good deeds are physical manifestations of changed hearts, demonstrating proof to others about our devotion to God.

Surrender

Today I will pray for help if I am still struggling with sin patterns, and I will seek out other Christians who are further along in their faith.

Stand Strong

If anyone comes to you and does not bring this teaching, do not receive him into your house or give him any greeting.

2 JOHN 1:10 ESV

In today's world a lot of people—and even churches—are compromising the gospel of Jesus Christ in an effort to "build bridges." Increasingly, society views Christians who strictly adhere to biblical teachings as intolerant haters. But the Scriptures warn about entertaining false doctrine that denies core aspects of Christianity. Jesus possesses divine and human attributes. He is uncreated and eternal. He came to earth, died on a cross, and rose from the dead on the third day. He ascended to the Father and is now reigning in power and authority. Though we can show respect and humility to people whose viewpoints do not embrace Christian doctrine, we must not water down important gospel truths or fail to articulate our true beliefs.

Surrender

Today I will pray for boldness and courage in sharing my faith with others.

Truth Test

Beloved, do not believe every spirit, but test the spirits to see whether they are from God, for many false prophets have gone out into the world.

1 JOHN 4:1 ESV

There are quite a few false prophets running around today. During the 2020 Presidential Election and the COVID-19 pandemic, I watched a variety of YouTube pastors, evangelists, and other influencers spouting different "prophecies." Quite a few claimed to have received divine messages from God, but their predictions never manifested. After all the dust settled, most did not take responsibility for speaking false claims, and they simply moved on with ministry as usual. This led to great disillusionment among followers who'd put faith in these teachers. We must always test prophecies against the Word of God and the fruit they produce and seek the guidance of the Holy Spirit to determine actual truth. False prophecies spoken in desperate times can do serious damage to the body of Christ.

Surrender

Today I will seek guidance from the Holy Spirit in my daily life and ask him to lead me into all truth.

Time Well Spent

Count the patience of our Lord as salvation, just as our beloved brother Paul also wrote to you according to the wisdom given him.

2 PETER 3:15 ESV

It's hard to look around at the world in its current state and not feel hopeless. In my home state of Minnesota and several other states, the Enemy's agenda seems to be prevailing through the passing of evil legislation and the advancement of godless agendas. You, too, may be asking yourself, *How much worse does it have to get before God intervenes?* For people who have wasted years in bondage to addiction and other sinful behaviors, there's an even greater sense of urgency to use the remaining time wisely. The apostle Peter wrote the above verse when he was close to death, fervently urging people to get right with God. Our Lord, in his infinite patience, has extended the remaining days in hopes that all people will repent and turn to him.

Surrender

Today I pray God will give me a drive and urgency to reach lost people.

Final Countdown

They will give account to him who is ready
to judge the living and the dead.

1 PETER 4:5 ESV

Many live like there is no God. The Bible illustrates similar scenarios. For instance, the people of Noah's day thought he was a demented old man and mocked his ark while carrying on with business as usual. I was a lot like that before I began seeking Jesus; I assumed I was saved by a little prayer recited as a child, considered myself darned near immortal, and didn't give eternity much thought. Every night spent at the bar was just another wasted opportunity where I could pretend I was important, receive empty validation from strangers, and numb reality. Thank God I was driven to repentance before losing my life. Everyone on earth will eventually face judgment and give an account of how they spent their time. Let's live in a way that will ensure Jesus says, "Well done, good and faithful servant!"

Surrender

Today I will pray for God's help with living righteously.

Practice Control

We all stumble in many ways. And if anyone does not stumble in what he says, he is a perfect man, able also to bridle his whole body.

JAMES 3:2 ESV

The Bible teaches that controlling our little old tongue will enable us to manage every other aspect of life. Isn't that amazing? Past wounds can definitely hinder communication strategies. I've struggled with sarcasm, criticism, and judgment in an effort to protect myself from being hurt, and the early years of married life suffered because of my insatiable need to say everything without thinking—or more importantly, without praying. After becoming born again, I finally learned to take matters to God first. Many problems were resolved simply by prayer. Words can be time wasters, weapons, or lifelines. Before speaking, ask yourself if what you're about to say is helpful, true, or encouraging. If not, reconsider. Use your powerful tongue to speak life.

Surrender

Today I will pray before I speak and ask the Holy Spirit to guide and direct my words.

Forever Faithful

Jesus Christ is the same
yesterday and today and forever.
HEBREWS 13:8 ESV

My life has been a revolving door of people. Can you relate? A few solid folks stick around for a lifetime, but most just pass through for a season. As a kid, I always felt insatiable with an overwhelming fear of people leaving. Abandonment wounds and dysfunctional homes will often have that affect. Strings of boyfriends, superficial drinking buddies, and so many friends and coworkers came and went. Some were genuine, many failed me, and in some cases, I was the betrayer. Through it all, I searched for one thing. Someone who would never leave, fail, or forsake me. But I wouldn't find what I desired in any human being, only in Jesus Christ. Today's verse displays proof of the Trinity, the nature of Jesus, and his divine attributes. Jesus is eternal, never changes, and is the only one who can offer true stability.

Surrender

Today I will place total trust in Jesus, who never changes.

Twisted Scriptures

There are many who are insubordinate, empty talkers and deceivers, especially those of the circumcision party.

TITUS 1:10 ESV

Many destructive teachings seek to poison and corrupt the true message of the gospel of Jesus Christ. We find New Age schools of thought running rampant, along with cults, religions that reject Jesus' deity, and occult practices claiming to be harmless. Even Christian doctrine can swing to wild extremes. Some hyper charismatic churches preach "Jesus lite," where all roads lead to heaven and the Lord is simply a brother who "gets you," while other more orthodox types insist on works-based piety and self-sacrifice to earn our way to God. Sometimes it's hard to sort everything out. We must seek God's wisdom through daily prayer, diligent study of the Scriptures, and guidance from the Holy Spirit.

Surrender

Today I will pray for discernment to recognize false teachings that could lead me astray.

Have No Fear

[Grace] now has been manifested through the appearing of
our Savior Christ Jesus, who abolished death and brought
life and immortality to light through the gospel.

2 TIMOTHY 1:10 ESV

Sharing the message of Jesus with others can be profoundly
difficult for many. We all have our excuses for keeping our
faith to ourselves, but perhaps the most common involve fear
of all kinds: of rejection, of judgment, of embarrassment, or
of being unable to answer follow-up questions. The thought
of witnessing to strangers along with pressure to "save the
world" can prompt people to feel overwhelmed and resort
to giving up completely. Being open to sharing how Jesus
changed your own life is always a good place to start. Few
can argue with an honest and heartfelt disclosure, and
your witness can bear a powerful impact on someone else.
Something supernatural happens when we share the gospel.
Pray for opportunities, and then be willing to let God use
you in new ways.

Surrender

Today I pray for God to place someone in my path who
needs to hear my faith story.

Until the End

As for you, brothers,
do not grow weary in doing good.
2 THESSALONIANS 3:13 ESV

An old Billy Joel song claims that "Only the Good Die Young." This wry statement seems to illustrate the futility of pursuing a life of integrity, an endeavor that is growing increasingly quaint in our wicked world. But be encouraged, for we don't have to pursue righteousness all alone. When we confess Jesus Christ as Lord and Savior and repent of our sins, the desire to abandon our sinful life becomes overwhelming, allowing righteous living to come naturally. But staying on the straight path requires the help of other Christian warriors. There is strength in numbers, and together we gird each other up to live a life of righteousness and integrity. There is a great reward up ahead.

Surrender

Today I will pray for strength and godly connections to help me do good work for the kingdom.

Avoid Offense

Good sense makes one slow to anger,
and it is his glory to overlook an offense.

PROVERBS 19:11 ESV

We all have reasons to get offended. Someone cuts you off in traffic. A friend overlooks your important milestone. No one greets you in church on Sunday. Your husband doesn't notice your new outfit. Offense is the devil's most effective weapon against Christians because it causes us to turn inside ourselves to ponder our own thoughts and perceived injustices, and this results in a natural withdrawal from people. Offense takes us outside God's will and can lead to rash decisions. The pastor says something you don't agree with, so you leave the church. Your husband fails to make you feel special, so you withdraw affection. A friend doesn't like your recent social media post, so you get back at them. Instead of overreacting to slights, give grace, seek God, and let things go.

Surrender

Today I will ask God to reveal when I'm becoming offended and will quickly repent.

The Big Boss

Work willingly at whatever you do, as though you were
working for the Lord rather than for people.

COLOSSIANS 3:23 NLT

Working for a miserable boss can drain the life from
you. Since turning sixteen, I've toiled under many different
leaders. Some were great, some horrible, but most were just
average. Forever searching for better working conditions,
I meandered from retail to food service to telemarketing
to sales. Though each position had pros and cons, a simple
shift in my own attitude did much more to improve my work
situation than changing jobs, leaders, or coworkers. Instead
of dwelling on circumstances and people, focus on God and
do everything with him in mind. It is generally unwise to
leave a position until he opens a new door or until a strong
calling is unmistakable. Control what you can, make changes
as needed, and bring glory to God through your work.

Surrender

Today I will pray for God to help me focus on him rather
than on people and circumstances.

Rejoice Always

Whatever happens, my dear brothers and sisters, rejoice in
the Lord. I never get tired of telling you these things,
and I do it to safeguard your faith.

PHILIPPIANS 3:1 NLT

Praising God is easy when the seas of life are calm. It was
easy to do so during the early days of deliverance from
addiction. But when disaster struck, and my marriage hung
by a thread, praising him was much harder. Rejoicing in the
Lord became nearly impossible as my natural urge to control
the situation consumed me. It wasn't until I had exhausted
all human effort that I finally trusted Jesus with the outcome.
While in the worst of circumstances—a prison cell—the
apostle Paul reminded the Philippians to continually rejoice.
When we are grounded in the eternal hope of life with Jesus,
our earthly problems will fade into the background as we
trust him in hard times.

Surrender

Today I will ask God to help me focus on him with gratitude
when life is difficult.

Take a Stand

Don't act thoughtlessly,
but understand what the Lord wants you to do.

EPHESIANS 5:17 NLT

Too many Christians are shirking their responsibility to represent Jesus. Many claim to be Christ followers but are really more like casual fans. Simply plastering your car with Jesus bumper stickers, posting faith memes on social media, and going to church on Sunday won't cut it. Being a Christian can be lonely, uncomfortable, and difficult. Our faith may force us to be the odd person out, to refuse certain invitations, or to speak up even though everything inside us wants to clam up and run away. We are all expected to take a stand for righteousness if we want to stake our claim as true followers of Jesus. There may be temporary discomfort, but we must stay focused on the great reward waiting in heaven.

Surrender

Today I will pray for boldness and courage
in my Christian walk.

Pursuit of Jesus

Christ has truly set us free.
Now make sure that you stay free,
and don't get tied up again in slavery to the law.

GALATIANS 5:1 NLT

Tullian Tchividjian, the grandson of Billy Graham, wrote a book entitled, *Jesus Plus Nothing Equals Everything*. If you're a reformed striver like me, you might struggle with this and wonder, *But what must I do?* Here's the answer: Believe in the one (Jesus) who was sent, repent of your sins, and accept him as Lord and Savior. Put your total trust in him and submit to his lordship. That's it. Evidence of true conversion will come through the fruit of a changed life along with a desire to pursue holiness. This won't happen overnight, but a natural desire to follow him, reject sin, and quickly repent will grow over time. There is nothing extra, no other works you must perform. Surrender to him, be obedient to the Holy Spirit, and do the next right thing.

Surrender

Today I will pray for Jesus to set my schedule and help me to be obedient to his leading.

All You Need Is Love

Three things will last forever—
faith, hope, and love—
and the greatest of these is love.

1 CORINTHIANS 13:13 NLT

The book of 1 Corinthians contains the popular "love chapter." Many people pluck the well-known words from their Bibles and weave them into their wedding ceremonies. It is indeed beautiful and enduring to consider the bedrock pillars of faith, hope, and love, as well as their ability to transcend any obstacle. If we look at the text in greater context, we see that the apostle Paul had just wrapped up a teaching on spiritual gifts. He seems to be saying that the spectacular gifts are indeed great—prophecy, tongues, discernment, and all that jazz—but don't lose yourself in the quest for only the snazzy supernatural goodies. Without love, everything else becomes pointless. Knowledge, talents, and resources are helpful attributes, but every one of them is meaningless without the bedrock of love.

Surrender

Today I will ask Jesus to help me do everything in love.

Plenty for Everyone

Accept each other just as Christ has accepted you
so that God will be given glory.

ROMANS 15:7 NLT

Too many people are all about self-promotion. We seek exposure for our ministries, are forever on the hunt for more followers, and pray for open doors and growth opportunities. Maybe we even get jealous or offended when we watch fellow brothers and sisters in Christ thriving and receiving promotion. *Why not me?* we silently whine. This type of behavior is extremely distasteful to God. Instead of feeling slighted because we aren't getting our prayers answered speedily, we must join forces with others in the body of Christ. There is more than enough blessing for everyone. We should support, build up, and seek to elevate those around us. We are all in this fight together.

Surrender

Today I will pray for unity among the body of Christ.

Lead Fearlessly

Some were persuaded by the things he said,
but others did not believe.

ACTS 28:24 NLT

The apostle Paul devoted his life to evangelism, and even though he'd had a personal encounter with Jesus on the road to Damascus, many refused to believe his words. Think about it: If Paul, one of the godliest men in history, couldn't convert every nonbeliever, then what makes us think we won't sometimes face rejection too? Fear of rejection forces many into silence. The good news is that we aren't called to do the work of the Holy Spirit. We're only tasked with sharing the gospel and our testimony, and then we need to leave the heavy lifting to God. Some will be moved to believe through our words, we may plant a seed for others that someone else will harvest later on, and some will simply reject the message. Keep witnessing and don't let fear of failure become a stumbling block.

Surrender

Today I will ask God for courage to share my faith with others.

Bearing Witness

"I am praying not only for these disciples but also for all who will ever believe in me through their message."

JOHN 17:20 NLT

The verse following today's passage says it all: "May they be in us so that the world will believe you sent me" (v. 21). Jesus devoted his earthly ministry to preparing the way for lost people to find salvation through his death on the cross. He is the only way to eternity in heaven, and there is great hope in the prayer that he offered during his last hours. He pleaded to the Father not only on behalf of the disciples but also for all future Christians. Our job as believers is to point others to Jesus through our witness. Through our testimony or some other work of the Holy Spirit, people will decide. We should do everything we can to help others understand who Jesus is so they can decide to follow him.

Surrender

Today I will be intentional about pointing others to Jesus.

The Real Thing

Immediately he began preaching about Jesus in the synagogues, saying, "He is indeed the Son of God!"

ACTS 9:20 NLT

When Jesus does something amazing in your life, you just can't keep quiet about it. August 22 was the day the Lord showed up in my moment of complete desperation, repentance, and surrender and radically transformed me. Because I had tried to stop drinking in so many ways but failed, I knew I'd just experienced the real thing. I've been free almost twenty years now. The Bible tells us to "taste and see that the LORD is good" (Psalm 34:8). Haven't you had enough of the world and solutions that don't last? Take your burdens, lay them at the feet of Jesus, and surrender. Once you stop trying to fix things on your own, he will meet you with his marvelous grace.

Surrender

Today I will stop striving, ask Jesus for help, and believe.

Willing for Wellness

One of the men lying there had been sick for thirty-eight years. When Jesus saw him and knew he had been ill for a long time, he asked him, "Would you like to get well?"

JOHN 5:5–6 NLT

My father battled alcoholism for many years. It started innocently, as addiction often does—a few beers at night, little nips of brandy on the weekends. But years of subtle imbibing soon grew into an enormous stronghold. Doctors, friends, and recovery groups with hands outstretched wanted to come alongside him to help. His answer? "I don't have to do anything." Jesus didn't just immediately heal the sick man lying by the pool of Bethesda in the fifth chapter of John, though he could have. First, he gauged the man's willingness by posing a question. "Would you like to get well?…Pick up your mat, and walk!" (vv. 6, 8). Jesus stands ready to help and heal, but he wants your buy-in. Are you ready? Do everything you can and trust Jesus to do the rest.

Surrender

Today I will become willing to let Jesus come in and transform my life.

Pursue the Lost

"In the same way, there is joy in the presence of God's angels when even one sinner repents."

LUKE 15:10 NLT

Being on fire for Jesus can make us want to save the world. This is not a bad thing, but the overwhelming nature of it can bring discouragement and inertia. My pastor, though, once delivered a sermon about the importance of saving lost souls and offered a simple solution to this challenge. He encouraged the church to pray for God to lay specific individuals on our hearts, just three souls at a time. Spiritual assignments like this can feel intimidating, but each of us is uniquely suited to speak into the lives of others by sharing our life experiences and special gifts. Who are the lost people God wants you to impact? Ask the Holy Spirit for inspiration, write down the names you receive, and begin to pray for the ones the Spirit reveals to you. When someone on your list becomes a Christian, replace them with a new prayer subject. You'll be amazed by what Jesus will do.

Surrender

Today I will pray for God to reveal the names of three people who need prayer.

Stay Faithful

"Everyone will hate you because you are my followers.
But the one who endures to the end will be saved."

MARK 13:13 NLT

Looking back at the last few years, the world's attitude
toward those who love Jesus and strive for biblical
principles is far more negative than it was even a decade
or so ago. When we heed warnings about persecution, the
persecution we picture is the dangerous kind that can lead
to imprisonment or even death. But Jesus also warns us of
the small-scale things, like losing a good friend over faith or
being singled out in an opinionated group of atheistic peers.
The pain of rejection can make it hard to remain faithful.
Scripture tells us to expect times of persecution for our
Christian faith. As our culture grows increasingly deceived
by the Enemy, it should not be a surprise that followers of
Jesus will face more opposition. Be encouraged. You will be
rewarded for your steadfast dedication to God.

Surrender

Today I will pray for strength and courage to face the
difficult days ahead.

Release the Hurt

"No, not seven times," Jesus replied,
"but seventy times seven!"

MATTHEW 18:22 NLT

Forgiving people who have harmed us does not come easily for most. There is often a natural tendency to seek retribution or the desire to inflict pain on the offender unless the other party expresses regret or apology over their actions. But pardoning those who have hurt us is a biblical mandate with no limits. Choosing to forgive doesn't mean you're endorsing the behavior or are required to have a relationship with your adversary. But by releasing them from any grudge you hold against them, your anger and bitterness will begin to fade, and healing can begin. This action will bring miraculous freedom by lifting the enormous burden that comes from harboring an offense.

Surrender

Today I will pray for help to forgive those who have harmed me.

Cheerful Giving

"Bring all the tithes into the storehouse so there will be enough food in my Temple. If you do," says the LORD of Heaven's Armies, "I will open the windows of heaven for you. I will pour out a blessing so great you won't have enough room to take it in! Try it! Put me to the test!"

MALACHI 3:10 NLT

Different perspectives on the biblical principal of giving or tithing are everywhere. Some argue it's simply a musty Old Testament mandate that disappeared when Jesus abolished the law by his death on the cross while others say Jesus intends us to continue tithing today. Personally, I don't think you will ever go wrong with contributing to the functioning of your church family. Members of the body of Christ should be invested in the financial support of their house of worship. Missionaries need support, pastors must get paid, and programs require cash to operate. However, you should not feel forced or mandated to give. Pray and ask God to show you how and when to open your wallet. Any amount is acceptable, as long as you give it freely and from a tender heart.

Surrender

Today I will pray for God to show me where I can best use my money and how he wants me to support my local church.

Finish Strong

"This is what the LORD of Heaven's Armies says:
All this may seem impossible to you now,
a small remnant of God's people.
But is it impossible for me?
says the LORD of Heaven's Armies."

ZECHARIAH 8:6 NLT

As a kid, I gained a reputation for making many grand plans but rarely seeing them through to the end. I struggled to finish college, was famous for embarking on massive diet programs but quitting after a few days, and, most notably, was constantly swearing off alcohol "for good" and failing. That is, until I met Jesus. Everything we attempt through our own self-will is ultimately destined for failure. Human strength sags, and willpower fades. Only by surrendering to Jesus and hitching your wagon to him can you truly finish the most important task of all.

Surrender

Today I will ask Jesus to help me avoid procrastination and allow him to set my priorities.

Rock Solid

The Sovereign LORD is my strength! He makes me as surefooted as a deer, able to tread upon the heights.

HABAKKUK 3:19 NLT

As I've said before, I try not to let the snow derail my running goals in wintertime. In order to find sure footing on the slippery streets, I have to wear those special traction cleats I've spoken of so fondly. Without them, I could easily take a tumble onto icy pavement or face plant into a snowbank. Like those special shoe coverings made just for the Minnesota elements, reliance upon God makes us sure-footed in a world that is constantly trying to sweep us away from the foundation of biblical teachings. As we grow in our understanding of the Lord, we will rise above our circumstances and learn to trust even when things don't make sense. Get into the Bible and let it plant steady truth into your heart. No matter what may be going on today, keep your eyes fixed on Jesus, and he won't allow you to stumble.

Surrender

Today I will ask the Lord to keep me on the path that leads to his perfect will.

Walk Humbly

No, O people, the LORD has told you what is good, and this is what he requires of you: to do what is right, to love mercy, and to walk humbly with your God.

MICAH 6:8 NLT

My grandma June was born on June 8. She loved fiercely and struggled with being a widow as well as losing her beloved sister and later her cherished grandson. I remember her devotion to God, her command of the piano, the hymns she adored, and how she once told me, "The sky always weeps on Good Friday." She was imperfect as we all are, but deep down, she wanted with all her heart to serve Jesus. Today's verse describes a few things that Grandma June understood are extremely important to Jesus: showing mercy, being humble, and pursuing righteousness. If we are steadfast in these areas, we will do well.

Surrender

Today I will pray for God to help me to do what is right and to become merciful and humble.

Seek Truth

"God is Spirit, so those who worship him must worship in spirit and in truth."

JOHN 4:24 NLT

Addictions often come packed with extremes, rash decisions, and the tendency to emotionally react before pausing to evaluate long-term consequences. Even in sobriety, I'm guilty of this. One week I'm a strict carnivore; the next thing you know, I've become a vegan. I've been in all sorts of churches from the most conservative of the Reformed to the most unconventional charismatic tent revival. I've explored deliverance ministry and listened politely to people's accounts of miraculous healings. Though I have personally received a filling of the Holy Spirit, I remain cautious about signs and wonders. Be careful about any church that goes to extremes in ministry. It's hard for a new Christian to wade through everything, but one thing is clear—the truth is quiet. Let God show you the way.

Surrender

Today I will pray for discernment and ask God to lead me into all truth.

September

First Things First

Jesus spoke to the people once more and said, "I am the light of the world. If you follow me, you won't have to walk in darkness, because you will have the light that leads to life."

JOHN 8:12 NLT

My name is Melissa, and I am an alcoholic." I just couldn't get the words out. Being coaxed to label myself a struggling drunkard when I was bone dry was a major stumbling block for me in recovery meetings. Totally redeemed and no longer living the chaos of active addiction, the words felt hollow and disingenuous. When we accept Jesus, we are transformed from the inside out and stop living and behaving as we did in the past. Jesus called himself the great I AM. If we truly want to be his followers, we must identify ourselves first and foremost as sons or daughters of King Jesus. We find true identity in him—not in a diagnosis, title, role, or label. Live from this reality, and you will never be the same again.

Surrender

Today I will reflect on my most important identity—a son or daughter of King Jesus.

Choose Well

"Today I have given you the choice between life and death, between blessings and curses. Now I call on heaven and earth to witness the choice you make. Oh, that you would choose life, so that you and your descendants might live!"

DEUTERONOMY 30:19 NLT

For years I blamed my addiction on things I believed were outside of my control. I held responsible my family of origin, the anxiety I battled, and other misfortunes for my messed up life. Although these circumstances definitely contributed to my alcohol abuse, every time I got drunk, I knew exactly what I was doing and could have chosen otherwise. I had other options but instead obeyed my flesh because I wanted to be popular, liked, and recognized. Truly, no one forced me into anything. Sin always feels good in the moment but comes with a bitter aftertaste. Godly living requires sacrifice but always involves a blessing.

Surrender

Today I will ask for the wisdom to make good choices.

Wise Counsel

Don't turn your back on wisdom, for she will protect you.
Love her, and she will guard you. Getting wisdom is the
wisest thing you can do! And whatever else you do,
develop good judgment.

PROVERBS 4:6–7 NLT

I wish I'd known about the book of Proverbs back when
I was a teenager. I could've saved myself much pain and
heartache. In Scripture we read that God was pleased when
Solomon prayed for wisdom above all other things. In
contrast, as a young person, I instead asked for a boyfriend
and a pair of downhill skis. Solomon wrote the majority of
Proverbs while under divine inspiration to offer instruction,
wisdom, and understanding. If you have struggled with
making good choices, don't despair, the Bible is full of wise
counsel that will faithfully speak directly into your life.
Proverbs is a smart read for people of all ages.

Surrender

Today I will ask God for wisdom and discernment to make
wise choices.

Get Ready

Since we are living by the Spirit, let us follow the Spirit's leading in every part of our lives.

GALATIANS 5:25 NLT

The statistics about addiction counseling are not encouraging. The dropout rate is high, and only a small percentage of people who manage to complete a treatment program will remain sober for a full year after discharge. So what works? Research shows that early improvement is the biggest predictor of overall outcome. People who seek out services with a willingness to change have a great chance of success. The Holy Spirit helps us get ready. He is at work in our hearts, bringing conviction, usually for a long time before we are desperate enough to act. Become willing to address what is holding you back today. Maybe you're battling addiction or some other stronghold. In whatever case, surrendering to God will help you take the next steps.

Surrender

Today I surrender to God's will and ask him to help me stop bad habits.

Respect Yourself

Humble yourselves under the mighty power of God, and at the right time he will lift you up in honor.

1 PETER 5:6 NLT

Sometimes we give people a lot more power than they deserve. Maybe it's the woman who stole your husband, the boss who is making life miserable, or the friend who betrayed you. Putting things into proper perspective can dramatically change how we view people and the world. Every human is just one person, and we all have opinions, feelings, and motives; we all fight battles and have issues. Even the richest and most powerful influencer is still subject to the normal laws of humanity and will struggle with fears, regrets, and disappointments. We will all die someday. Be careful not to allow anyone to use their position to diminish you. No one but God holds your destiny.

Surrender

Today I will find encouragement in remembering that I am as valuable as any other human being.

Give Grace

Follow peace with all men, and holiness,
without which no man shall see the Lord.

HEBREWS 12:14 KJV

It's easy to let petty slights consume us. At times, we can become so deeply affected by other people's actions and opinions that simply being around human beings is almost crippling. Some of the Enemy's favorite weapons are resentment and bitterness. If he can succeed in getting us so fixated on the actions of others, then our sensitivity to God's voice grows weak, and Satan secures a foothold. Bitterness blunts the freedom of the Holy Spirit and causes us to isolate ourselves from others. The cure for most interpersonal conflicts is to offer grace and avoid over-personalizing the matter. Steer clear of resentment and unforgiveness and you will stay in God's will. Instead of being a prisoner to someone's actions, repent, forgive, and do your best to reconcile.

Surrender

Today I will pray about any resentments I have been holding.

Touchy Topic

Flee from sexual immorality.
All other sins a person commits are outside the body,
but whoever sins sexually, sins against their own body.

1 CORINTHIANS 6:18 NIV

As a child, I was woefully unprepared for the enormous amount of brokenness I would invite into my life through casual sexual relations. My mother was extremely uncomfortable about the topic, so all the information I gained came secondhand from friends. Deep down, I believed that giving my body to a man would bind us together. Truly, this did happen—but not in the way God had intended. Rather than renewing a covenant promise designed for marriage, I formed ungodly soul ties. My pattern of blackout binge drinking dovetailed into sexual immorality, and I frequently made bad decisions. The Lord deeply desires that we honor him with our bodies. If you have struggled in this area, there is no condemnation for you. Repent, turn from sin, and step into a new beginning.

Surrender

Today I will seek forgiveness for any sexual immorality and ask God to free me from shame.

True Brotherhood

Greater love hath no man than this,
that a man lay down his life for his friends.

JOHN 15:13 KJV

Most people I knew from my partying days were superficial drinking buddies. The crew that waited at the bar each night made me feel important. Our time together involved binge drinking, chasing guys, and lots of superficial talk, nothing deep. When I became sober, my bar friends disappeared, and we didn't speak anymore. In fact, we had nothing in common. How about you? Does your current social circle truly have your back? Jesus is the ultimate confidante. He suffered persecution, ridicule, and torture, yet laid down his life for each of us. No friend of this world can even come close to the incredible wellspring of security we find in Jesus. Don't worry about the quantity of friendships you have; instead, seek quality relationships with Christians who want to honor God and share their life with you.

Surrender

Today I will take stock of my circle of friends and ask God
to bring people who will truly love and support me.

Use Your Words

"What about you?" he asked.
"Who do you say I am?"
MATTHEW 16:15 NIV

My daughters once attended a youth conference hosted by our church, and one of the evangelists who spoke proposed a witnessing technique that resonated with many in attendance: "Try asking people, 'Who do you think Jesus is?'" For some reason, this felt easier than more direct approaches like, "Do you know where you're going when you die?" or "Do you have a personal relationship with Jesus Christ?" Over the following week, my daughter managed to strike up conversations about Jesus and share her relationship with him with five different friends. Anything that can help us become more comfortable with leading others to God is helpful and worthy of our time and effort. It is so much better to speak up than to stay silent and expect someone else to take that risk.

Surrender

Today I will take a risk and ask someone about their thoughts about Jesus.

What's the Point?

"Meaningless! Meaningless!" says the Teacher.
"Utterly meaningless! Everything is meaningless."

ECCLESIASTES 1:2 NIV

My life leading up to the day Jesus delivered me from addiction was a series of experiments to find meaning. I tried seeking the approval of people, setting goals, getting degrees, being recognized, and achieving the usual American dream of a family, home, and stable job. My efforts paid off temporarily, but restlessness and dissatisfaction always returned. Everything is hopeless unless your life is anchored in Jesus Christ. When we approach the world with a kingdom mindset, we realize that the earth is not our home. We live to please God and find great hope in knowing our ultimate destiny is in heaven with him. Only then can we grasp the true meaning of life.

Surrender

Today I will pray for an eternal mindset and remember that everything in this life is temporary.

Check Yourself

"When you give to the needy,
do not let your left hand know
what your right hand is doing."

MATTHEW 6:3 NIV

Addiction is a selfish problem that involves making an idol out of a substance or behavior. We become completely turned within, prisoners in our own little worlds of problems and pain, offense and shame. We are rendered powerless and ineffective in this state, essentially useless to God. When we become sober, it's common to shift to the other extreme and turn ourselves into service machines—volunteering at every possible opportunity, shouting "Jesus!" from the mountaintops, attempting to save the world. Giving to others is an essential piece of the Christian life, but it is essential that we do it from a heart that is right with God. Are you helping out for his glory or just seeking a reward? Check your motives, then pray for God's guidance in doing the next right thing.

Surrender

Today I will pray for pure motives.

Live with Purity

The wages of sin is death,
but the gift of God is eternal life
in Christ Jesus our Lord.

ROMANS 6:23 NIV

Addictions naturally give way to other sinful behaviors. Thinking back to my bartending days, my steady diet of vanity, pride, greed, and sexual immorality was completely opposed to righteous living. Being immersed in that dark lifestyle produced a breeding ground for new levels of sin every day. Though God condemns all of it, disobedience comes in different categories. Some are minor, like gossiping or letting a curse word slip out, but others, like addiction and sexual immorality, are much more serious and can shorten a person's life through overdose, diseases, accidents, or suicide. Wrong choices can quickly lead us down a destructive path. Choose the new life waiting for you in Christ Jesus and you will find freedom from sin and death.

Surrender

Today I will pray for help with making choices that led to life and peace.

God before People

*What shall we say about such wonderful things as these?
If God is for us, who can ever be against us?*

ROMANS 8:31 NLT

People-pleasing is an extremely hard habit to break because it is so highly reinforcing. Living in harmony with others feels good and makes life easier, and getting praise brings a sense of belonging and acceptance. For many years, I dismissed my own feelings and values in order to keep the peace and to avoid upsetting others. I kept my opinions private and only shared what was safe, repeatedly staying silent in situations where I needed to speak up. Conflict avoidance took a toll until finally this counterfeit version of myself became intolerable. Now, instead of trying to pacify people, I seek God's will. People-pleasing might feel good in the moment, but abandoning godly values in the process is never worth it.

Surrender

Today I will seek God's will and pray for help to stop my people-pleasing behaviors.

Exercise Good Judgment

The temptations in your life are no different from what others experience. And God is faithful. He will not allow the temptation to be more than you can stand. When you are tempted, he will show you a way out so that you can endure.

1 CORINTHIANS 10:13 NLT

Relapse is a common occurrence in recovery circles. Counselors and addiction specialists warn newly sober folks to avoid certain people and the slippery places that can become hotbeds of temptation. Initially, you must guard your new recovery like you would a delicate infant. Don't allow anything to threaten your precious sobriety; treat it like fine china that must be protected. Be careful and plan ahead, and don't subject yourself to situations that hold the power to derail your commitment. But know this. Jesus Christ is your most powerful ally in the recovery battle. Sponsors, therapists, gurus, and coaches don't have anything on the King of kings. Start each day by asking him to help you avoid temptation.

Surrender

Today I pray Jesus will help me avoid temptation and will open my eyes to potential risks.

Walking Wounded

Come quickly, LORD, and answer me,
for my depression deepens.
Don't turn away from me, or I will die.

PSALM 143:7 NLT

Addiction is a dead-end road that often spits us out bruised and battle worn. People who simply "put down the drink" but don't receive inner healing will remain broken vessels that God will not be able to fully use. Many people get into recovery, seek therapy, obtain coping skills, and learn how to function at a surface level, but the wounds that caused them to seek numbness from substances are still buried. Coping techniques help, but for complete heart restoration, you must seek Jesus for soul therapy. Pray and spend time soaking in his presence. Practice listening to his gentle voice without urgency. He will unearth your broken parts layer by layer and show you how to achieve wholeness.

Surrender

Today I will pray for Jesus to reveal any unresolved brokenness and to show me how to heal.

True Identity

"No longer shall your name be called Abram,
but your name shall be Abraham;
for I have made you a father of many nations."

GENESIS 17:5 NKJV

Back in my bartending days in the '90s, the tavern crew christened me "Mel." Mel had dyed red hair, slammed four beers to perform DJ duties, and tossed bottles of tequila like the stars in the movie *Cocktail*. But she was a fraud. Though I liked her for a season, I knew she wasn't really *me*. When we become free of addictive vices and surrender to Jesus, we can allow him to shape our true identity, rather than the one the world has forced upon us. We die to the opinions of others and walk in freedom, knowing we are pleasing to our heavenly Father. Stop caring about the impressions of others and become the person God created you to be. There's nothing in the world quite like it.

Surrender

Today I will ask God to help me walk in my true identity.

It's Not about You

I have been crucified with Christ. It is no longer I who live, but Christ who lives in me. And the life I now live in the flesh I live by faith in the Son of God, who loved me and gave himself for me.

GALATIANS 2:20 ESV

One of my biggest problems used to be thinking everything was about me. I was hypersensitive about how others acted, assuming any of their mood fluctuations were my fault. Having a disagreement with someone was agony to my fragile identity. As I took a stronger stand on biblical issues, things only grew worse. I had drawn a line in the sand about my true Christian beliefs, and now others were pushing back. One day in church, a thought dropped: *It's not about you. It's about Jesus.* My main objective then became seeking God's wisdom and being obedient. I began pointing people to the Bible instead of trying to defend myself. The opinions of man didn't control my mood once I became focused on crucifying my flesh and allowing God to fight my battles.

Surrender

Today I pray to be free from fear of man and obedient to the Holy Spirit.

Devil in Disguise

No wonder, for even Satan disguises himself
as an angel of light.

2 CORINTHIANS 11:14 ESV

Boys, music, and beers. These three things, though not inherently harmful, were my vices. For example, my first boyfriend was not an evil person, just a misguided kid with family issues who stumbled onto my path. The heavy metal music we poured into our brains wasn't necessarily evil, but we used it to fuel our desire to rebel and flip the bird to the establishment. Beer is not an evil thing in and of itself either, but the devil knew how to use it for evil, and when we drank it in abundance every weekend, it was like pouring gasoline on a fire. The Enemy knows our weaknesses and our neediness. He's a master at offering half-truths and encouraging "harmless" disobedience that's just a *little* wrong. But beware. Satan's greatest weapon is deception, and agreeing with his lies always brings disaster in the end.

Surrender

Today I pray that Jesus will open my eyes to the devil's attempts to deceive me.

Crucify the Flesh

> People who aren't spiritual can't receive these truths from God's Spirit. It all sounds foolish to them and they can't understand it, for only those who are spiritual can understand what the Spirit means.
>
> 1 CORINTHIANS 2:14 NLT

Although I don't drink anymore, I still occasionally frequent places that serve alcohol. Once, my husband and I were enjoying dinner at a supper club, and as we were finishing our meal, a DJ began to set up karaoke equipment. One thing about me is that I never refuse an opportunity to sing in public. While I waited for my turn on stage, a man nearby struck up a conversation. We briefly discussed faith, and he mentioned being a Christian. "I've been here partying for the past six hours!" he added. I was reminded of the conviction I used to feel about my wrongdoings after nights of binge drinking at the local tavern. The apostle Paul describes two types of Christians: one group walking in spirit and truth and the other living for self and entering heaven by mere inches. To truly be like Jesus, we must die to ourselves, crucify our flesh, and welcome the conviction of the Holy Spirit.

Surrender

Today I will ask Jesus to help me live righteously so that I do not fall back into old sinful behaviors.

Kingdom Riches

[God made] known to us the mystery of his will,
according to his purpose, which he set forth in Christ.

EPHESIANS 1:9 ESV

When I consider the greatest gifts I've ever received, I think of my children, the engagement ring my husband presented when he popped the question, and a pair of used downhill skis my parents scrimped and pinched to put under the Christmas tree. But Jesus Christ has promised us believers a reward that far surpasses anything this world could offer—spending eternity with him when our time on earth ends. Compared to infinity with Jesus, anything we struggle with today seems insignificant, and even the most thrilling experiences pale in comparison. When day-to-day life gets burdensome or unfulfilling, it's time to reflect on the incredible price Jesus paid for our salvation. It is sometimes easy to gloss over this unbelievable act of love and surrender.

Surrender

Today I will remember the great price Jesus paid so that I could spend eternity with him.

Exclusive Rights

"Salvation is found in no one else, for there is no other name under heaven given to mankind by which we must be saved."

ACTS 4:12 NIV

These days, proposing the exclusivity of Jesus Christ is almost considered hate speech. With hundreds of different world religions, how can Christianity possibly be the only right one? Simply because the Bible says so, and the Bible is factually accurate and can be trusted. No other religion can effectively prove beyond reasonable doubt that its leader died and then resurrected, as the Christian faith can. Our entire belief system hinges upon this fact, with loads of historical evidence, archaeological findings, and thousands of manuscripts to back up its claims. C. S. Lewis once said, "Christianity…, if false, is of no importance, and, if true, of infinite importance. The one thing it cannot be is moderately important."[4] Though research, facts, and data can be helpful, people need the Holy Spirit to come into belief. Without his power illuminating our minds and removing deception, we will remain in darkness.

Surrender

Today I pray the Holy Spirit will illuminate hearts and minds about the power of the gospel.

---

4   C. S. Lewis, *God in the Dock* (Grand Rapids, MI: Wm. B. Eerdmans Publishing Co., 2014), 102.

Justice for All

"Everyone who calls on the name of the Lord will be saved."

ROMANS 10:13 NIV

For most of my life, I haven't felt part of the gang. I wasn't too athletic or talented, and other kids weren't particularly drawn to me. I was usually the last one picked for team sports and wasn't always invited to the hottest birthday parties. If this was also your experience, take heart in knowing God does not play favorites. He desires that everyone comes to saving belief in him and promises to never turn away someone who seeks the truth with a sincere heart. Sometimes we make Christianity so complicated when, at its core, it's really very simple. Confess your sins, believe in Jesus, and ask him to take control of your life. You will never regret it.

Surrender

Today I will confess my sins and ask Jesus to take control of my life.

Name above All

God exalted him to the highest place
and gave him the name that is above every name.

PHILIPPIANS 2:9 NIV

Many so-called Christians are just fine with talking about God. God feels safe, universal, and palatable. Most people even claim a belief in God. But which god are they talking about? A couple of years ago, I attended a class at church that was marketed as a way to learn how to create a dialogue and share faith with Muslims. Quickly it became clear that the underlying aim of the course was to promote interfaith relationships through affirming similarities but stopping short of sharing the gospel of Jesus Christ. There is power in the name of Jesus, and without an understanding of him, there is no belief in the one true God. Jesus is God. To suggest anything less is wrong, antichrist, and blasphemy.

Surrender

Today I will remember there is absolute power in the name of Jesus and in no other name.

Spread the News

"My prayer is not for them alone. I pray also for those who will believe in me through their message."

JOHN 17:20 NIV

Perhaps the greatest biblical command is for Christians to go and make disciples, leading others into a saving relationship with Jesus Christ. Jesus made a number of requests during his famous High Priestly Prayer in the seventeenth chapter of the book of John. At first glance, it may appear as if he is speaking only to his disciples, but the verse also applies to all who would come after the early church. We must never tire of sharing our faith in Jesus, our very purpose for walking this earth is to save souls and lead others into a relationship with the living God. We do this through our unique witness, personal testimony, and specific words and actions as the Holy Spirit leads us.

Surrender

Today I will look for opportunities to share my faith story with someone else.

Live Righteously

We know that the law is good
if one uses it properly.

1 TIMOTHY 1:8 NIV

My habitual pattern of drunk driving led to several run-ins with law enforcement. When I was disobeying God, I had a great deal of shame from living in a way that was grievous to the Holy Spirit. Rules and laws like the Ten Commandments are good because God gave them, but some people think they no longer apply because of Jesus' atoning work on the cross. Consider his words: "Do not think that I have come to abolish the Law or the Prophets; I have not come to abolish them but to fulfill them" (Matthew 5:17 ESV). Though we are not bound to many cultural rules or rituals outlined in the Bible, the moral code of right and wrong still applies. When Spirit-filled Christians disobey this code, we will naturally feel conviction, grief, and a strong need to repent. Obedience is not about being perfect or acting right; rather, it is having a genuine desire to please and serve God. When we fail, he is there to clean us up and get us back on the right path.

Surrender

Today I will pray for a hunger and thirst to pursue God's righteousness and follow his ways.

Be Fearless

He said to me, "My grace is sufficient for you, for my power is made perfect in weakness." Therefore I will boast all the more gladly about my weaknesses, so that Christ's power may rest on me.

2 CORINTHIANS 12:9 NIV

I have struggled with fear most of my life, tracing back to childhood feelings of rejection that came with conflict or disagreement. I found it difficult to be direct, assert myself, or even have an opinion that upset or bothered anyone else. For a long time, I thought prayer would eradicate fear, but even after seeking the help of spiritually gifted people, I still struggled. As I've grown spiritually, avoiding the truth has become impossible, and I am unable to stay silent about beliefs, ideas, or movements that oppose God. I wasn't magically delivered from fear, but God showed me how to walk through uncomfortable situations. Speaking the truth isn't easy, but Jesus will reward you for honoring him. As you learn to trust, your faith will grow, and you'll become bolder knowing he is right by your side.

Surrender

Today I pray for courage and strength to defend what matters to God.

Rescue Mission

He lifted me out of the slimy pit, out of the mud and mire;
he set my feet on a rock and gave me a firm place to stand.

PSALM 40:2 NIV

One of the lowest moments I recall from my drinking days was stumbling home from the bar one night and falling into a swamp. For what seemed like hours, I lay drifting in and out of consciousness and unable to get up. It was humiliating, and I remember promising myself—again—that this would be the last time I got drunk. Though I still drank again for another year, God used each relapse and fall from grace to bring a crushing conviction that would eventually result in repentance and a sincere desire to never drink again. Willingness is key. Are you ready to leave behind your sinful, chaotic, destructive life? Call upon the name of Jesus, and he will faithfully come to the rescue. Addiction grows progressively worse and often results in an early death. Seek Jesus for healing and trust that he is fully able to deliver you.

Surrender

Today I will trust that God is able to save me from any situation.

Backsliders Beware

I heard the voice of the Lord saying,
"Whom shall I send? And who will go for us?"
And I said, "Here am I. Send me!"

ISAIAH 6:8 NIV

It takes most addicts a while to get sick of being miserable. Many of us go to great lengths to find a way to keep drinking and drugging even when our behaviors are inviting patterns of destruction. For four painful years, I vacillated between following the leadings of the Holy Spirit and then falling into sin again. Then one night I got drunk and experienced a long blackout followed by unbearable shame. The next morning, everything had changed, and the enormity of my sinful ways flattened me. I repented of every wicked act and asked the Lord to set my feet on a new path. I have not turned back. Decide today what needs to change in your life and become committed to seeking God. He is faithful to hear your desperate cry.

Surrender

Today I pray for conviction and the power to follow God's ways without backsliding.

The Good Book

I saw the dead, great and small, standing before the throne, and books were opened. Another book was opened, which is the book of life. The dead were judged according to what they had done as recorded in the books.

REVELATION 20:12 NIV

Books are some of my best friends. As a young girl, devouring the entire Nancy Drew mystery series kept me sane in a home of dysfunction. Getting lost in a novel was like stepping into another world. Today's verse paints an eerie picture: those who did not accept the Lord standing before the great white throne. Jesus, who came to earth to make a way for all to be saved, will judge them. Instead of seeing them through the atoning work of Christ on the cross, God will evaluate them by their own deeds. Believers whose names are written in the Book of Life will not suffer this terrible fate, and God will count them righteous because of their faith in Jesus. Take this verse seriously and accept the free gift of salvation today.

Surrender

Today I pray my name will be found in the Book of Life and that the Lord will show me any areas that need repentance.

God's Story

"They triumphed over him by the blood of the Lamb and by the word of their testimony; they did not love their lives so much as to shrink from death."

REVELATION 12:11 NIV

Some people have fantastic testimonies marked by near-death experiences, visions of heaven, or miraculous healings that restored their dying bodies. But most testimonies are average accounts of regular people who have overcome challenges, unbelief, and everyday issues because of the cross of Christ. The Enemy would love for people to keep their mouths shut about the transforming power of Jesus so that he can plant condemning and deceptive thoughts into your head: *You're not special. You're boring. No one cares about your struggles.* Your testimony belongs to God. Don't disappoint him by making it about yourself. Everyone's story will uniquely resonate with certain people. Honor God by using what he has brought you through for the good of others.

Surrender

Today I will pray for boldness in sharing my testimony as well as for opportunities to bless others.

October

Lonely Road

"If anyone comes to me and does not hate father and mother, wife and children, brothers and sisters—yes, even their own life—such a person cannot be my disciple."

LUKE 14:26 NIV

When we leave addiction behind and begin pursuing a new life with God, not everyone will celebrate our conversion. As a newly sober person, I tried to come clean to a family member about ways I felt they had harmed me and how their own addiction had impacted me. Unfortunately, the other person did not welcome nor validate my need to pursue healing. Sometimes this happens, but dealing with our own internal baggage is still important regardless of how the others involved may receive it. The further we progress in our journey with Jesus, the more difficult it becomes to tolerate sin, evil, and ungodliness. You may have to create new boundaries with people or, in some cases, even sever communication with someone who does not respect those boundaries. Find encouragement in knowing the Lord will bless you for placing him first.

Surrender

Today I pray for the wisdom to discern healthy relationships and boundaries.

Divine Intervention

They said, "Come, let us build ourselves a city, with a tower that reaches to the heavens, so that we may make a name for ourselves; otherwise we will be scattered over the face of the whole earth."

GENESIS 11:4 NIV

Have you ever thought you didn't need God and were perfectly capable of managing life on your own? The culture described in Genesis 11 certainly did, believing their own self-will would supply everything. After falling into idol worship, they constructed a tower to call down the gods, but the Lord God blocked the rebellious plan by confusing their language and making communication impossible. When I was in bondage to addiction, God sometimes stepped in and used consequences like arrests, financial problems, damaged relationships, and intense inner turmoil to stir in me a desire to change. Is the Lord trying to get your attention today?

Surrender

Today I will pray for open eyes and ears to perceive God's messages.

Here I Am

"I looked for someone among them who would build up the wall and stand before me in the gap on behalf of the land so I would not have to destroy it, but I found no one."

EZEKIEL 22:30 NIV

Some people confuse the nature of God with his mind. We know from Scripture that God's nature doesn't change. He is the same yesterday, today, and forever. However, we see countless situations in the Bible where he does indeed relent or change his mind in response to prayer. Many people don't believe petitions have the power to influence anything. I can honestly say that intercessory pleas offered by others saved my marriage. When all else failed, God in his divine mercy directed my husband and me to a gifted prayer team who stood in the gap for us, interceding and rebuking Satan so we could move forward. Prayer calls God's will down from heaven and releases it on earth. He is looking for people to stand in the gap and intercede today. Are you willing?

Surrender

Today I will pray for God to use me to intercede on behalf of a person or situation.

Master the Flesh

I know that good itself does not dwell in me, that is, in my sinful nature. For I have the desire to do what is good, but I cannot carry it out.

ROMANS 7:18 NIV

Even after being born again, we continue to war with a human nature, often behaving in opposition to the Holy Spirit. Fasting is one of the best ways to crucify the flesh. I used to despise the very thought of this kind of depravation, and honestly, the last thing I wanted to give up was my beloved coffee. After much resistance, I embarked on a seven-day fast. Although it was difficult, it also deepened my relationship with Jesus in ways I never dreamed. Abstaining from food and other distractions created space to get serious about prayer and the Bible. If you want to pour gasoline on your prayers, fasting is that accelerant. Ask God what he wants you to give up and devote additional time to prayer. Strip away anything that blocks you from him, and you'll hear his voice more clearly.

Surrender

Today I will seek the Lord's will about fasting in my life.

Stand Firm

"God blesses you when people mock you and persecute you and lie about you and say all sorts of evil things against you because you are my followers."

MATTHEW 5:11 NLT

The Bible tells us that others will persecute us for following Jesus, and in some parts of the world, Christians are killed or imprisoned for their faith. Though most Americans haven't suffered intensely for their beliefs, our culture has grown increasingly dark and hostile toward followers of Christ. People of faith are being targeted, with those who believe in the God of the Bible open to ridicule and even arrest for peaceful protests and public prayer. Now more than ever, we must stand firm, call on Jesus, and trust him to come to our aid, if not in this life, then absolutely when we stand before him in the next. Commit to yourself and to God that you will never bow down to anyone but him.

Surrender

Today I will pray for strength and courage in the face of mounting hostility toward Christians.

Best Friends

The LORD replied,
"My Presence will go with you,
and I will give you rest."

EXODUS 33:14 NIV

Sometimes I am a little jealous of the relationship Moses and God enjoyed. Even though Moses struggled and doubted, he regularly went into God's presence and saw the Lord face-to-face, like a trusted friend. In the verses preceding today's verse, Moses had just pleaded with the God Almighty, saying he could not go on alone unless he could be assured of the Lord's presence. Have you ever felt that way? Just desperate for more of God and a deep awareness of him? That promise given to Moses still stands today through Jesus. Find encouragement in knowing he is the closest friend you will ever have. Call on him in times of trouble and rest in knowing he hears you. Take time to soak in his love today.

Surrender

Today I will find peace in knowing Jesus will never leave or forsake me.

Judge the Fruit

"By their fruit you will recognize them.
Do people pick grapes from thornbushes,
or figs from thistles?"

MATTHEW 7:16 NIV

I tend to become captivated by brilliant Bible teachers. I'm just so impressed by their mastery of Scripture and their ability to apply it that I sometimes fail to see their humanness. I started following an influencer who could recall verses accurately through the power of the Holy Spirit. While his knowledge was indeed impressive, his character defects and scorn for people he perceived beneath him soon overrode his profound intellect. The condescension, arrogance, and shaming tactics he used to witness were extremely off-putting and unhelpful. Intellectual abilities are useless without a genuine desire to teach others through the love of Christ. As the apostle Paul warns in 1 Corinthians 13, without love, lofty words are nothing but a clanging cymbal.

Surrender

Today I will pray for Jesus to help me show love to everyone I meet.

True Blood

A man of many companions may come to ruin,
but there is a friend who sticks closer than a brother.

PROVERBS 18:24 ESV

I have an older brother. He is a great guy, but our six-year age difference meant we weren't very close as kids. I always wished for a sister who would be more like a best friend. Many of us who've battled addictions struggle with finding true, meaningful relationships that can extend beyond the barstool or the crack house. Take heart in knowing the Lord wants to bring new connections into your life—people who truly have your back and want to share life on a deep and meaningful level. Superficial drinking and drugging buddies are not what Jesus had in mind for you, so even if it's hard, find the resolve to let them go. Real Christian friends can be closer than family, bringing honest fulfillment, refining, and joy to your life.

Surrender

Today I pray that the Lord will bless me with true Christian friends.

True Love

"As the Father has loved me, so have I loved you. Now remain in my love."

JOHN 15:9 NIV

Perhaps you've been hurt by someone who promised to love you. Maybe it was a parent, a friend, a spouse, or all three. Most people have experienced pain and rejection in personal relationships. Sometimes we place unfair burdens on others by expecting perfection, completion, and adoration from broken humans who are unable to give it. People do the best they can with what they have. Although my earthly father loved me, he battled demons from his own childhood dysfunction. My husband harbored baggage from his family just like me, and forcing him into a flawless knight-in-shining-armor role was simply not realistic or fair. Looking to people for unconditional adoration will always end in disappointment. Only God is capable of offering the perfect love our souls crave.

Surrender

Today I will rest in the arms of the Father and ask him to help me believe that his love for me is true.

Obey the Spirit

The mind governed by the flesh is death,
but the mind governed by the Spirit is life and peace.

ROMANS 8:6 NIV

Believing in Jesus and being born of the Holy Spirit is the greatest decision you will ever make. But your new conversion doesn't mean you won't battle sin or the desire to disobey. When I was radically freed of alcohol addiction, I was instantly relieved of craving, obsession, and mental preoccupation, which is very uncommon and completely amazing. However, I still struggled in other areas, continuing to battle insecurity, control, and pride for years. The most difficult stronghold to overcome was fear. Some afflictions will endure until Jesus returns, but take heart in knowing our weaknesses are made perfect in him. We must pray daily for a fresh filling of the Holy Spirit and to surrender to the will of God. As we crucify our flesh and obey the Spirit, we will gain greater mastery over our sin nature.

Surrender

Today I will pray for God to help me follow the Holy Spirit
and resist the desires of my flesh.

Clean Slate

"I will forgive their wickedness
and will remember their sins no more."

HEBREWS 8:12 NIV

Satan loves to bring frequent reminders about our past sins and failures. You might be having a great day with God, and out of nowhere, the Enemy shoots a fiery dart into your mind in the form of a bad or condemning thought. Maybe it's a memory of something you did while drunk or high, a time you lost control of your emotions, or some other regretful thing. The devil knows our weak spots and how to sow seeds of doubt and insecurity, always looking to bring guilt and shame. The voice of God is stronger, speaking love, joy, peace, and gentleness. Rest assured that once you have repented and submitted to Jesus, he promises to wipe away your sins forever.

Surrender

Today I will rest in knowing that once I have repented, I am delivered of sin.

Solid State

The Lord is faithful, and he will strengthen you
and protect you from the evil one.

2 Thessalonians 3:3 niv

Many people have extreme and irrational fear about relapse. While standing strong against temptation is important, there is no need to become paralyzed by worries about caving to temptation. When I decided that I was done with alcohol forever, something inside shifted. I had never before expressed a firm commitment, always leaving open a crack the door to drinking. When God knew I was serious after my final relapse, he moved on my behalf—completely lifting alcohol's allure. Though I still had to approach life with some measure of caution, I had peace about it, realizing Jesus would bring deliverance in every situation where the devil attacked. Get this down into your spirit. The Enemy has no power over you once you repent of sin and begin following Jesus.

Surrender

Today I will ask Jesus to help me avoid temptation.

Humble Yourself

He gives us more grace. That is why Scripture says:
"God opposes the proud but shows favor to the humble."

JAMES 4:6 NIV

Everyone knows a person who always insists on being the leader, who needs to be right, and who has a terrible time listening to others. Many of these overbearing types shoot themselves in the foot with their attempts to secure first place. Humble people lead quietly by example, are good listeners, and have no desire to prove themselves. Often we perceive pushy, take-charge, prideful folks as heavy hitting go-getters in the business arena and those displaying humility as weak or passive. But remember, the kingdom view is completely different than that of the world. When Jesus came to earth, he served others free of self-promotion, and he taught his disciples to do the same. He was gloried by the Father for his obedience. We should follow his example.

Surrender

Today I will pray for God to remove pride and teach me to be humble.

Just Call Me Jeffrey

God created mankind in his own image, in the image of
God he created them; male and female he created them.

GENESIS 1:27 NIV

When I was around seven, I went through a tomboy phase.
I told my mother to call me Jeffrey and refused to wear pants
without a zipper. Mom rolled her eyes and went along with
my nonsense, and my gender quirk quickly passed. These
days, when a young girl or boy goes through a masculine
or feminine phase, it's becoming increasingly common in
our society to reinforce that behavior. The Bible tells us that
God created two sexes: male and female. We are his image
bearers and God desires that we embrace and celebrate the
body he has given us. If you are struggling with this, please
know there is no condemnation. God loves you, and Jesus
can bring freedom. Seek help from strong believers and a
Christian therapist who can offer support.

Surrender

Today I will praise and thank God for making me perfectly
and wonderfully in his divine image.

Beautifully Simple

You have been my hope, Sovereign LORD,
my confidence since my youth.

PSALM 71:5 NIV

I am forever grateful to my spiritual mother, Marge. She is the reason I accepted Jesus all those years ago in a church basement at the conclusion of Vacation Bible School one summer. I said a very simple prayer and received the Holy Spirit. But almost instantly afterwards, the Enemy began to attack my newfound belief. Years later, I'd fall into binge drinking and promiscuity, and Satan whispered: *You never really meant that prayer.* For a long time after experiencing radical freedom from addiction, I wondered how I'd been spared death after so many close calls. Today, I know the Holy Spirit never left me after my childhood conversion. You don't have to do anything fancy to make it work. Just repent of your sins and believe, and his presence will endure forever. It is by faith through his grace that we receive Jesus.

Surrender

Today I will rest in knowing that I received the Holy Spirit
when I first believed.

My Defender

The LORD is my strength and my shield; my heart trusts in him, and he helps me. My heart leaps for joy, and with my song I praise him.

PSALM 28:7 NIV

Are you always feeling the need to win people over through persuasion or manipulation? The habit of getting defensive can be an attempt to deal with the feeling of never truly being heard or understood. This tendency can be a side effect of the falsehoods we've heard other people say about us or lies we've accepted. We start to think the world is against us and that we're fighting behind enemy lines. The constant need to prove yourself to others is exhausting and creates self-absorption that makes serving others difficult. Pray for God to reveal any remaining self-defeating patterns. Ask for his help with honoring him and decide not to worry about outside opinions. He is the only one worth pleasing.

Surrender

Today I will ask God to help me stop defending myself and seek only to please him.

Quality Time

Laziness brings on deep sleep,
and the shiftless go hungry.

PROVERBS 19:15 NIV

Newly sober people are often cautioned to avoid too much idle time. Sitting around doing nothing can definitely give the Enemy an open invitation. The word *boredom* may imply having nothing interesting to do or look forward to, but something greater than a simple lack of stimulation is going on. Persistent apathy has a more sinister cause—the feeling of worthlessness or emptiness. Just finding "stuff" to fill the days—mindless TV watching, surfing the internet, scrolling social media—is not enough; our pursuits must be God-honoring. Activities that enrich your walk with Jesus and further a kingdom purpose are crucial. Finding true identity in him is a sure-fire way to avoid temptation. As you grow into the person God has created you to be, you will feel a new sense of purpose and self-worth.

Surrender

Today I will pray for Jesus to show me fulfilling and God-honoring ways to spend my time.

Anger Management

My dear brothers and sisters, take note of this:
Everyone should be quick to listen,
slow to speak and slow to become angry.

JAMES 1:19 NIV

I used to have terrible road rage, quickly flying into a fit of anger if someone cut me off or drove too slowly. I also had great difficulty controlling emotional responses even when I wasn't driving. As the Lord dealt with this, I became aware of my failure to effectively represent Christianity to the rest of the world during times of stress and high emotion. Venting about my problems to others only seemed to magnify them and was not helpful. After much prayer and introspection, I realized the only answer was surrendering to the Holy Spirit during intense moments, and I began using everyday situations as a way to build my control muscle. Long lines, angry people, and disappointments of all kinds can become opportunities to demonstrate love, tolerance, and patience.

Surrender

Today I will pray for the Holy Spirit to change me from being quick-tempered to having the love of Jesus.

Proceed with Caution

Cast all your anxiety on him
because he cares for you.

1 PETER 5:7 NIV

Mental health diagnoses have skyrocketed in recent years, with doctors prescribing to countless Americans pharmaceutical drugs to treat depression and anxiety. Experiencing bouts of low mood or anxious feelings is a normal part of life. But psychiatric conditions are intensified when normal human emotions become opportunities to pop a pill rather than seek an underlying cause. Doctors widely overprescribe pharmaceutical drugs to treat minor emotional disturbances when often the answer is simple. Seek Jesus first for guidance in choosing doctors, therapists, and medications. Next, let the Bible help you adopt an attitude of thanksgiving and gratitude. Lifestyle modifications like getting more exercise, being in nature, adopting relaxation techniques, getting better sleep, and a consuming a healthy diet take more effort than swallowing pills but pay great rewards with little to no negative side effects.

Surrender

Today I will ask God to guide me to the best solutions for depression, anxiety, and other life struggles.

It's That Simple

Whether you eat or drink or whatever you do,
do it all for the glory of God.

1 Corinthians 10:31 niv

Overeating was a battle I fought for many years. My
childhood involved bingeing on junk food to cope with
anxiety and fear, and as a teen, I wavered between starving
myself and consuming enormous quantities of food. Until
I was delivered from blackout drinking, I was unable to
practice moderation, and my weight swung wildly between
being obese and being borderline underweight. For thirty
years, I was not eating for the glory of God. Instead, I
attempted to use food to numb emotions, generate a
dopamine rush, and deal with boredom. Pursuing health is
an important part of a recovery lifestyle. If we can eat and
drink for God's glory, we will be minding the body God
has given us. Focus on clean, whole foods from nature and
minimize packaged or boxed junk. Eating natural foods
supplies essential nutrients that put the brakes on overeating.
It's that simple.

Surrender

Today I will ask God to help me make healthy choices in
food and drinks.

Honor Your Body

Do you not know that your bodies are members of Christ himself? Shall I then take the members of Christ and unite them with a prostitute? Never!

1 CORINTHIANS 6:15 NIV

My sex education was limited to a brief, dry talk in junior high health class along with the whisperings and speculations of girlfriends at slumber parties. I never dreamed of asking my mother questions about the "deed" or considering God's ideas about it. Rather I viewed sex as a rite of passage that I should hurry up and experience. Never in my wildest dreams did I consider the enormous consequences of joining my body with someone outside of marriage. This thoughtless teenage decision invited a plethora of pain, disappointment, and insecurity. It may seem outdated and countercultural, but God has important reasons for designing sex to be shared only within a marriage between one man and one woman. Here, it is a beautiful and incredible gift where two really become one flesh. Sex outside of marriage is an act of lust, and you can't build a foundation on that.

Surrender

Today I will thank God for the gift of sex to be enjoyed in a marriage and will ask forgiveness if I've sinned in this area.

Money Matters

The love of money is a root of all kinds of evil.
Some people, eager for money, have wandered from
the faith and pierced themselves with many griefs.

1 Timothy 6:10 NIV

While in bondage to addiction, I had no control over my finances or my ability to spend and save wisely, but I still carried my desire to be rich. We all need money to function in society, and having wealth is not a sin. But an obsession with getting rich is very displeasing to God, and if your desire for prosperity overrides your pursuit of him, it is time to rethink your priorities. The Bible also says, "Where your treasure is, there your heart will be also" (Matthew 6:21 NIV). How do you obtain your money? Where does your money go? What do you value? Regardless of what you claim, your bank account will reveal the truth. Make sure to earn your money honestly, steward your finances well, use them to help others, and assist in the advancement of the kingdom.

Surrender

Today I will ask God to help me spend wisely and to prioritize my money.

It Pays to Be Wise

"Do not store up for yourselves treasures on earth,
where moths and vermin destroy,
and where thieves break in and steal."

MATTHEW 6:19 NIV

I used to frequent a wildly popular coffee chain every single day. Justifying my habit was easy—so many others were also locked into the drive-through along with me, and five bucks per visit didn't seem too bad. Slowly, God convicted me of this behavior by highlighting news stories about unbiblical causes the company supported, and he even making the coffee taste terrible to me after awhile. When I calculated my annual expenditures for premium coffees, my eyes were opened. Ultimately, I quit my expensive coffee habit and began putting the cash into savings. Pray for God to guide your finances and to help you use them for his glory. Your bank account reveals your priorities. Time and money are your two biggest commodities, and both are a gift from God.

Surrender

Today I will pray for God to show me how he wants me to spend my money.

Out of Order

Dear children, keep yourselves from idols.

1 JOHN 5:21 NIV

The world offers many remedies for addiction problems: treatment centers, medications, recovery groups, sober coaches, and therapies of all kinds. Secular approaches can teach useful coping skills, and connecting with a Christian therapist to help process problems is undoubtedly useful. But many seek help *backward*—believing that worldly things will treat the root cause of addiction. Like any obsession, the drink or drug becomes first place, and successfully overcoming this sort of idol worship requires repentance. Yep, that crusty old church word that feels so condemning to many is a necessary step to freedom. Seeking forgiveness from Jesus Christ will be the key to escaping bondage. He will faithfully guide you to the right people and places to assist your recovery journey.

Surrender

Today I will sincerely repent of anything I've placed before God and submit to his authority.

Greatest Gift

"Very truly I tell you, it is for your good that I am going away. Unless I go away, the Advocate will not come to you; but if I go, I will send him to you."

JOHN 16:7 NIV

After the Resurrection, Jesus spent forty days with his disciples and appeared to many others. But Jesus' departure from the earth was confusing. How could it possibly be good? As an amazing parting gift, he promised his very presence would return to the apostles through the Holy Spirit. The God-man they'd ministered with would no longer be physically present, but his Spirit was coming! The promise still stands today. Did you know that the moment we accept Jesus, we also receive the Holy Spirit, the presence of God? The third person of the Trinity is not an "it" or impersonal force. He, like the Father and Jesus, is also God. When we submit to him, he leads us in all truth.

Surrender

Today I will ask the Holy Spirit to give me wisdom and discernment and to lead me in all truth.

Power Play

> "The prince of the Persian kingdom resisted me twenty-one days. Then Michael, one of the chief princes, came to help me, because I was detained there with the king of Persia."
>
> DANIEL 10:13 NIV

If you're experiencing a delay from God, it is possible your prayer has been blocked. An invisible battle between good and evil still rages in the spiritual realm, and intense warfare can sometimes delay or hinder our petitions. The book of Ephesians discusses powerful angelic and demonic forces that are still active today. We must war in prayer daily, put on the full armor of God, and call upon supernatural assistance to penetrate the adversary's demonic hedge. Though Scripture tells us Daniel's prayer was stalled for three weeks, he did not give up until an answer came. Prayer involves warfare against dark forces, and we must not grow weary of persisting in the good fight of faith. Calling upon other Christian warriors when you've hit a roadblock can help bring the breakthrough.

Surrender

Today I will pray for warring angels to come and help push back the Enemy's hedge of darkness.

Morning Rejoicing

His anger lasts only a moment,
but his favor lasts a lifetime;
weeping may stay for the night,
but rejoicing comes in the morning.

PSALM 30:5 NIV

Every human has experienced a terrible day when everything went wrong. In the midst of a trial, nothing makes sense, and it may feel as though the suffering will never end. A fresh start the following morning often brings a new outlook and perspective. Sometimes, the trial is more persistent and may take months or even years to resolve. Even when we journey through dark seasons, peace will come through faith in Jesus, the passage of time, and a change of attitude. But even in the worst of cases—when the problem or hardship stays with us for the duration—comfort comes when we remember that those who trust in God will find rest and redemption in eternity. No earthly battle can overtake us when our confident hope remains in Christ Jesus.

Surrender

Today I will seek to learn and grow from my trials, knowing that I have eternal hope.

Attitude Shift

He spoke a parable to them,
that men always ought to pray and not lose heart.

LUKE 18:1 NKJV

We humans are such fickle beings. We have no problem praising God when he does our bidding, yet when prayers go unanswered or we are denied something, turning on him comes easily. Our pride and desire to control may prompt us to take matters into our own hands. Just a simple shift in perspective can lift a self-righteous attitude when circumstances are disappointing. When you're feeling frustrated with God, instead try adopting a posture of thanksgiving. Offer praise for everything—starting with the smallest blessing: The fact that you woke up today, can see, have hot water, have a roof over your head, have food to eat, enjoy the love of family and friends. Start magnifying what God has already provided, and you'll be amazed at the change of heart that follows.

Surrender

Today I will thank God for everything, even things that frustrate or confuse me.

Don't Delay

"Whoever hears these sayings of Mine, and does them, I will liken him to a wise man who built his house on the rock."

MATTHEW 7:24 NKJV

One day, I sensed God telling me to call a fellow mother from church. But I was busy, didn't have the time, and honestly didn't really feel like it. Telling myself I'd do it later, I kept procrastinating, but then time passed, and I rushed to pick my daughter up from school. On the way home, she told me her friend Anna had asked if she could come over to our house that night. I felt a sudden pang in my spirit; Anna's mother was the woman God had urged me to call! I quickly repented and thanked the Lord for a second chance, then I called Anna's mother, who shared about a medical scare in the family. Anna came over that evening, her parents got a much-needed breather, and everyone's mind eased a little. What is God asking you to do for him today?

Surrender

Today I will pray for God to help me obey when he makes a request.

Wasted Worries

Let the peace of Christ rule in your hearts, since as members
of one body you were called to peace. And be thankful.

COLOSSIANS 3:15 NIV

I wonder how many hours I've spent worrying about the
future, obsessing about a problem, or trying to predict how
an issue would resolve. Worrying wastes a lot of time and
energy but accomplishes nothing. After you've allowed
yourself ten minutes to ruminate, take that mental effort
and channel it to God. Imagine laying every burden down
at the foot of the cross. The shift in perspective is extremely
powerful, as he is the only one capable of making change
happen. The next time you are wrestling with a problem,
invite God into it. Redirect your obsession to petitions of
prayer. You'll feel better and will probably end up amazed by
what God will do.

Surrender

Today I will take my worries and bring them to God in
prayer.

Get Over Yourself

When pride comes, then comes disgrace,
but with humility comes wisdom.

PROVERBS 11:2 NIV

Want to know how to transform your life and entire way of thinking? Accept the fact your life does not actually revolve around you. Nothing in this entire world does. It revolves around God, doing his work, and furthering his kingdom. Maybe that sounds dull, but believe me, living from his will is as exciting as it gets. When you finally discover why he made you and begin walking on purpose, you'll never be the same again. Getting over yourself will enable you to stop feeling hurt, offended, and slighted by people and situations. You'll finally be able to stop personalizing everything and begin to walk in his divine purpose. Realizing it's all about Jesus is the key to true freedom. Get serious about finding out why he made you and start living your calling.

Surrender

Today I will ask Jesus to help me overcome the bondage of self and to become dedicated to fulfilling his purposes.

November

Flip the Script

Oh come, let us worship and bow down;
let us kneel before the LORD, our Maker!

PSALM 95:6 ESV

I really didn't feel like going to church this morning. The weather was crummy, I was tired, and I had a lot on my mind. Depressing thoughts like *I'm sick of fighting the same old battles* plagued me. The worship leader's efforts to cajole the congregation into praise made me resist even more. Then the pastor delivered the sermon and began to preach about testimonies of answered prayer within the body of Christ. As he called a young lady up to the stage to share her story, my spirit started to soar. Before long, I was shouting, "Hallelujah" and "Amen" and was filled with the pure joy of the Lord that comes from turning momentary troubles into praise. Shifting to a mindset of worshiping almighty God can completely transform your thinking, taking you from self-absorbed to focused on his awesome, transforming power.

Surrender

Today I will praise God no matter my circumstances or mood.

Lessons Learned

Cast your burden on the LORD, and he will sustain you;
he will never permit the righteous to be moved.

PSALM 55:22 ESV

Seasons of growth and refining can be difficult, and most of us want to hurry through the lesson to the blessing waiting on the other side. But the Lord does important work during times of confusion, hurt, or feeling far from him. When disaster struck my marriage, I wanted nothing more than to fix the problem and move on, but God had much to teach me. I could not hurry the process along; my meddling just caused more setbacks. I never imagined I'd gain such incredible insight during such a painful time, but I was forever changed through the refining work of God. He taught me a very important lesson—to shift my quest for human love to trust in him. Being able to finally put this revelation into practice was truly life changing.

Surrender

Today I will ask God what he wants to teach me while I am experiencing difficult seasons.

Let Hope Arise

May the God of hope fill you with all joy and peace as you trust in him, so that you may overflow with hope by the power of the Holy Spirit.

ROMANS 15:13 NIV

Even during the darkest days of addiction, I clung to a thread of hope. Through seemingly endless promises to change, something inside encouraged me to stand strong. It was the Holy Spirit who'd been there ever since the childhood prayer I recited at age nine. Take comfort in this, regardless of how many times you've fallen, God still has you. You woke up today, and that means you have another chance. The Enemy will whisper that it's over, that you've ruined things beyond repair. Ignore the devil's shaming attempts, yet keep in mind that you may not have another day. Let hope arise and become willing as you contemplate what God can do with a submitted life. Receive Jesus and the Holy Spirit today and watch your life transform.

Surrender

Today I will ask God for renewed hope that I can overcome challenges in my life.

His Agenda

"I tell you, whatever you ask for in prayer,
believe that you have received it, and it will be yours."

MARK 11:24 NIV

Wow, this verse sounds pretty slick, you may be thinking. *All I have to do is ask and believe and I can have whatever I want?* Could it really work, or is it all just New Age nonsense? Maybe you've heard of the Word of Faith movement, otherwise known as "name it and claim it." Proponents of this teaching believe they can ask for anything and it will materialize before their very eyes. This was certainly not what Jesus had in mind. Being a follower of Christ does not involve manipulation. While we must have faith and believe that God is completely able to do anything, we should seek wisdom first and always submit to his will. His plans for us are always so much better than anything we can manufacture alone. Believe big, step out in faith, and trust God with the results.

Surrender

Today I will ask God to keep me in his perfect will as I pray.

Love in Action

Everyone who believes that Jesus is the Christ is born of
God, and everyone who loves the father loves his child as well.

1 JOHN 5:1 NIV

When I was a clueless teenager, my biggest goal was finding
whatever keg party was happening that weekend. Church
life felt like a major drag. Bibles and obedience were the
furthest things from my mind, and the atmosphere of God's
house just felt dull and dry. So I turned to what I thought
was freedom—endless beers and approving glances to heal
my deep-seated insecurities. It would take years before I
realized that everything I coveted was killing me. After years
of letting the consequences of my own choices beat me into
submission, I realized the very thing I resisted was what
would ultimately save me: repentance and the pursuit of
Jesus. God's commands are not roadblocks to joy. Obedience
is the only way to become free from sin and a life lived in
bondage to self.

Surrender

Today I will ask for the power and desire to keep God's
commands.

Burning Your Influence

Fight the good fight of the faith. Take hold of the eternal life to which you were called when you made your good confession in the presence of many witnesses.

1 TIMOTHY 6:12 NIV

Don't burn your influence," my pastor often warns. Sharing strong opinions and stances on divisive issues before the time is right can cause other people to reject any wholesome teaching you're hoping to share. Until you've developed a relational base with someone, you should avoid topics like your opinions about certain political candidates, how you feel about hot-button issues, and your stances on heavily controversial things. After you've built a rapport, your conversation can progress to deeper levels. Laying all your cards on the table right away can cause people to write you off. The gospel message of Jesus Christ is something everyone should agree upon. Just be strategic with sharing so you don't ruin your witness.

Surrender

Today I will ask the Holy Spirit for guidance in setting boundaries with others.

Unanswered Prayers

When you ask, you do not receive,
because you ask with wrong motives,
that you may spend what you get on your pleasures.

JAMES 4:3 NIV

We've all been there. After praying, fasting, and sleepless nights—nothing. Begging and pleading, yet still no answers. Frustrated and confused, you're convinced God has rejected you. Or so it seems. If you're experiencing blocks in your prayer life, it might be time for self-examination. Are you holding on to a resentment or offense? Is there someone you're refusing to forgive? Are you failing to express gratitude? I've been there many times, and looking back, I can see how gratitude flowed from countless situations that didn't go as I'd hoped. I also see the pain I caused by forcing my own will and refusing to wait on God. If your heart is clear and unburdened and still you wait, it might be time to just thank God for unanswered prayer and to trust that he knows better.

Surrender

Today I will thank God for unanswered prayers.

Rivers of Peace

"Peace I leave with you; my peace I give you.
I do not give to you as the world gives.
Do not let your hearts be troubled and do not be afraid."

JOHN 14:27 NIV

Do you have problems that don't seem to get resolved? Stumbling blocks that show up in your path repeatedly? A life of addiction will prompt us to seek temporary peace in a bottle of alcohol or a joint, a geographical escape or a new relationship, but the sense of serenity is very short-lived. The world and its offerings will never quench the emptiness inside that only Jesus can fill. Distractions, vacations, possessions—they're fun for a while, but reality always waits around the corner. When we decide to live for Christ, we tap into a well of peace deeper than anything else. Life and its cheap thrills pale in comparison to the enduring rest of walking in relationship with God. Temporary fixes never satisfy for long, but the love and peace of Jesus will bring fulfillment like nothing else.

Surrender

Today I will lay down my burdens and ask Jesus to fill me with his peace.

Perfect Love

"If you, then, though you are evil, know how to give good
gifts to your children, how much more will your Father in
heaven give good gifts to those who ask him!"

MATTHEW 7:11 NIV

For years, I battled resentment and bitterness toward my
father. Dad wasn't like the guy from *Father Knows Best*
or *Leave It to Beaver*. He was a flawed man who did the
best he could with the hand he was dealt. He had personal
demons like many of us, yet I know he loved me to the best
of his ability. After experiencing imperfect parenthood
and a plethora of my own failures, I was finally able to
bury the hatchet and forgive. I also allowed Jesus to heal
negative memories and asked him to bring to mind positive
experiences I'd enjoyed with my father. People can't give
away what they don't have, and many parents are limited by
baggage from their families and unresolved issues. Whether
your earthly dad was a demon or a dream, it doesn't matter.
Your gracious heavenly Father loves you perfectly, and you
can trust him to never fail.

Surrender

Today I will release any resentments I hold against my earthly
father and ask God to shower me with his perfect love.

Pray It Forward

Confess your sins to each other and pray for each other so that you may be healed. The prayer of a righteous person is powerful and effective.

JAMES 5:16 NIV

I must admit I pray a lot of selfish prayers. I'm usually having one crisis or another, stressed about a situation, or preoccupied with some aspect of home or work life. The worst place for many addicts is inside our minds. The remedy for self-absorption is dedicated prayer for others. Most addicts will greedily accept a generous friend's offer of intercession—with no problem pouring our hearts out about our perceived issues—but have a hard time "praying it forward." Going to battle for others is transformational and will cause your own struggles to grow strangely dim as you war in prayer on behalf of another. Commit to asking at least one person each day about prayer needs, and the next time someone requests intercession from you, don't just agree halfheartedly, really do it.

You'll come to see that prioritizing others reduces your burdens and offers abundant blessings to both you and others.

Surrender

Today I will ask God to help me earnestly seek opportunities to pray for others.

The Power of Prayer

Pray in the Spirit on all occasions with all kinds of prayers and requests. With this in mind, be alert and always keep on praying for all the Lord's people.

EPHESIANS 6:18 NIV

Praying around others used to make me nervous. The first time my husband and I took the plunge and bowed our heads together, he'd just had surgery for appendicitis and had been prescribed a litany of nausea-producing drugs. Because he was experiencing intense pain, we knew he needed to take the pills, so we huddled close on the end of our bed, grasped hands, and hurriedly prayed for him. Praying alone can hold such power and bring comfort, even if God doesn't answer it when and how you want. But praying *together* can hold even more power. It can form a stronger bond between members of the body of Christ. If you only ever pray alone, I encourage you to join another believer and find fellowship as you seek God in prayer together.

Surrender

Today I'll ask God to give me a heart that desires putting prayer above my self-consciousness.

Priority Reset

"Watch and pray so that you will not fall into temptation.
The spirit is willing, but the flesh is weak."

MATTHEW 26:41 NIV

These days, Americans are more stressed out than ever.
With jam-packed schedules and tight deadlines, we forsake
relaxation and sleep to cram for meetings or juggle a million
activities for our children. Personally, I know that being
constantly maxed out and frazzled by too many demands
can invite relapse, and nonstop distraction and noise makes
hearing the still, small voice of God or the quiet promptings
of the Holy Spirit difficult. If this sounds familiar, it might
be time to take a look at your schedule and figure out where
the true priorities lie. Are there things you can trim from
the calendar? Do you need to start saying *no*? Are stricter
boundaries with others long overdue? Decide today to stop
overcommitting and agreeing to things you don't even want
to do. Make God your highest priority and then ask him to
set your appointments.

Surrender

Today I will look at my day-to-day activities and ask God to
set my schedule.

Trust the Spirit

*The Spirit himself bears witness with our spirit
that we are children of God.*

ROMANS 8:16 ESV

I can't tell you how many times I've been swept up by the latest trend or fad. More often than I care to admit, I've been charmed by a pastor's charisma instead of looking at the fruit he is bearing, casually followed false prophets before snapping back to reality, and even spent hundreds on books and teachings that did little more than increase my anxiety. These treks into no-man's-land were brief because the Holy Spirit faithfully brought conviction through a sense of unease. God wants to teach trust and reliance upon him, but as long as we're submitted to him with an obedient heart, he won't let us stray too far. You've got to surrender to God's will, pray for increased discernment, and allow him to reveal everything you need to see.

Surrender

Today I will ask God to deepen my discernment and to bring conviction when I am off track.

Tireless Pursuit

"'Because this widow keeps bothering me,
I will give her justice, so that she will not beat me down
by her continual coming.'"

LUKE 18:5 ESV

How many times have you asked God for something, decided God wasn't going to answer your prayer, and then thrown up your hands and concluded that prayer doesn't work? Don't just pray for a little while and then quit. First, ask God to show you any unrepentant sin that may be hindering you and request forgiveness. Continue to pray from a posture of surrender but don't be afraid to declare bold prayers. Countless times in the Bible, we see the dramatic impact of belief and faith demonstrated. How often do you plead with God to change someone in your life, maybe your spouse, children, or coworkers? Perhaps it's time to ask him to change *you*. My breakthroughs have always come through submission along with openness to personal correction and a desire to place a situation completely in God's hands.

Surrender

Today I will examine myself, ask forgiveness, and ask only for God's will to be done.

Take Action

Fear not, for I am with you; be not dismayed, for I am your God; I will strengthen you, I will help you, I will uphold you with my righteous right hand.

ISAIAH 41:10 ESV

When we are dealing with a crisis or tough situation, it is tempting to think that analyzing it will make the solution magically appear. Our minds tumble endlessly—sorting, dissecting, processing—but often leave us more distressed and fearful. Worrying is a form of inactivity that accomplishes nothing more than intensifying the problem. The more we dwell upon it, the more it grows like a fungus. Think of all the time you waste mentally obsessing about something you have no control over. Not only is it draining, but worry also depletes your very soul. Now take the effort and energy you would devote to rumination and redirect it to prayer. Ask God to show you the next right step and then follow through. You'll feel so much better after taking positive action.

Surrender

Today I will bring all my troubles and worries to God and ask him to guide me.

Perfect Will

"Your kingdom come, your will be done,
on earth as it is in heaven."

MATTHEW 6:10 NIV

I've got a lot of grand goals for the future. I'll bet you do too. Now that I'm fifty and my kids have only a few years of school remaining, my husband and I have shifted to empty nest plans. The condo in Florida, the RV tour of the country to spread the gospel, the cozy little home and library filled with books. But none of these ideas I have dreamed up will bear fruit unless God is the author. He knows better than we do, and allowing him to have control is the best decision we'll ever make. Things aren't always clear in the moment, but time brings illumination and insight. Pray for help to remain within his perfect will. If something isn't God's idea, it's never worth the pain and struggle it brings.

Surrender

Today I pray the Lord to redirect me when I get off track.

Not One and Done

Jesus replied, "You are in error because you do not know the
Scriptures or the power of God."

MATTHEW 22:29 NIV

When I was encouraging my husband to read the entire
Bible, I found that my nagging, pleading, and reminding
had very little impact, so I surrendered the matter to God.
Years later, the Lord brought another Christian into our lives
who invited my husband to a men's weekend retreat. When
he returned, he'd become hungry for the Word of God, and
his first, full read-through of the Bible ignited a desire in
him to learn more. Getting through the Bible once is great,
but we are never finished with God's Word. Reading and
meditating upon God-breathed verses fills us with truth
and power, and we become an anchor within a culture
beckoning sin and temptation every day. The Bible is the
bedrock of our sanctification journey, bringing knowledge
and opportunities for growth every day. Each reading is
a blessing, as the Holy Spirit delivers new revelation and
insight every time.

Surrender

Today I will pray for God to help me prioritize reading the
Bible every day.

Trust the Word

The heart is deceitful above all things,
and desperately wicked: who can know it?

JEREMIAH 17:9 KJV

What is your heart telling you to do? Trust it and do what you feel is best." We hear these platitudes a lot, and even in therapy sessions and addiction treatment groups. Some well-intentioned Christians also offer poor advice, suggesting "doing what feels right." But what if our hearts are completely misguided? Emotions are fickle things driven by countless circumstances—moods, physical health, the behavior of others, even the weather! Emotions are not a trustworthy truth barometer. Always seek God in prayer and make sure any decision aligns with the Bible. Don't rush, be patient, and wait on the Lord. Don't make any huge decisions without solid conviction or prior to seeking input from other solid Christians. Pray for guidance, do the next right thing, and proceed one step at a time.

Surrender

Today I will pray for wisdom and discernment with every decision.

The Greatest Story

> How can they call on him to save them unless they believe in him? And how can they believe in him if they have never heard about him? And how can they hear about him unless someone tells them?
>
> ROMANS 10:14 NLT

It's easy to assume everyone has already heard the good news, but that's not reality. It reminds me of an interview I once had with a former Muslim. His friend had become a Christian, and recognizing the sudden, dramatic change, he asked his friend about it. His friend was eager to tell him all the ways in which Christ had transformed his life. Never assume people have met Jesus, and keep in mind that something supernatural happens when we share the message of the gospel. The Holy Spirit does the work, so don't worry about having all the right answers or feeling like the responsibility of converting someone is yours alone. We grow in confidence through small steps of obedience. Start by leaving gospel tracts wherever you go and release the pressure to convince anyone to believe. Just share your testimony and let Jesus do the rest.

Surrender

Today I will pray for boldness and courage to share my witness with others.

For His Glory

"'In him we live and move and have our being.'
As some of your own poets have said, 'We are his offspring.'"
ACTS 17:28 NIV

Self-reliance runs rampant in our prideful culture. Many of us are helpless control freaks, believing we hold all the power, taking credit for good things, and striving relentlessly to create ideal outcomes. Committed to "living my best life," we plan, schedule, and set goals. Many ignore the reality that Jesus holds everything together and is the only reason we wake up, are breathing, and have the opportunity to live another day. Give credit where credit is due. Jesus calls the shots and decides whether we will live or die. Your heart and will are your greatest gifts, and Jesus wants both. If you're reading this, he's not finished with you! Decide to surrender today.

Surrender

Today I will thank God for the gift of my life and ask him to help me use it for his glory.

No Lost Causes

For this reason, since the day we heard about you, we have not stopped praying for you. We continually ask God to fill you with the knowledge of his will through all the wisdom and understanding that the Spirit gives.

COLOSSIANS 1:9 NIV

Are you believing for someone to come to Jesus? Behind many Christians who were once hell bound is a praying parent, grandmother, teacher, or friend. Marge Mahaney was my intercessor. For years, she petitioned the Lord on my behalf, even after I may have seemed like a lost cause. Throughout my rebellious teenage years and even as she watched me enter a marriage outside God's will, Marge begged God to intervene. You might be losing hope that a prodigal child, drug addicted friend, or hard-hearted spouse can still be touched by the love of Jesus. Don't despair! Your prayers *do* matter. Sometimes it takes years, but if we do not give up, we will see a reward—whether on earth or in heaven. Commit to praying for at least three people each day. Maybe you will be the reason they escape the flames of hell.

Surrender

Today I pray the Lord will give me endurance to keep praying for lost friends and loved ones.

Take Heart

Start children off on the way they should go,
and even when they are old they will not turn from it.

PROVERBS 22:6 NIV

The destructive force of active addiction ruins everything in its wake, leaving the addict to regret the harm they have done to children and other family members. Being captive to a substance can fool us into believing we have things under control and are functional, but this delusion is usually far from reality. Take heart! Whether your children are still small or have progressed into adulthood, it's not too late for God to redeem lost time, mend hearts, and bring healing. His sacrifice on the cross covers every single mistake. Pray for the Holy Spirit to take control of anyone who has been hurt in the wake of your addiction. We have all failed as parents, but our gracious heavenly Father can transform brokenness with his amazing power.

Surrender

Today I will forgive myself for mistakes I've made as a parent and ask Jesus to heal the brokenness in my damaged relationships.

Stay Focused

Our light and momentary troubles are achieving for us an eternal glory that far outweighs them all. So we fix our eyes not on what is seen, but on what is unseen, since what is seen is temporary, but what is unseen is eternal.

2 CORINTHIANS 4:17–18 NIV

So much can happen in any given twenty-four-hour period. We may start the day looking on the bright side only to become discouraged by slights and the cares of life. People who are walking around unhealed may cross our paths, projecting pain and darkness into our day. One of the greatest gifts you can give yourself is to stop reacting to other people's moods and behaviors. It's not about you anyway. Each person has different levels of baggage, and some lack coping skills to deal with it. Though life can definitely be challenging, we cannot let temporary struggles spoil our eternal focus. So much happens each day—many thoughts, feelings, ups and downs—but the hope of heaven remains constant. Stay focused on your eternal reward. Jesus is coming soon.

Surrender

Today I will keep my eyes on Jesus and the hope awaiting in heaven as I navigate the ups and downs of life.

Lean on Him

Three times I pleaded with the Lord to take it away from me. But he said to me, "My grace is sufficient for you, for my power is made perfect in weakness." Therefore I will boast all the more gladly about my weaknesses, so that Christ's power may rest on me.

2 CORINTHIANS 12:8–9 NIV

I've prayed so often to be delivered from fear of man. I've had intercessory teams go to bat, many hands laid, possible spirits cast out. But still the anxiety of facing potential rejection, hostility, or anger persists in certain situations. Many who have battled trauma, addiction, or dysfunctional childhoods can likely relate, and though we accept Christ, it does not mean all associated troubles will cease. The apostle Paul had afflictions too. Scripture tells us that he prayed three times for the thorn in his side to leave but was told his weakness was made perfect through reliance on Jesus. Instead of blaming God for not removing obstacles in your life, thank him for using them as growth opportunities.

Surrender

Today I pray for strength to continue working through problems and challenges with the help of Jesus.

Right Motives

"The earth will be filled with the knowledge of the glory of the LORD as the waters cover the sea."

HABAKKUK 2:14 ESV

A friend once told me about a pastor who was offered the chance to be interviewed by a famous television host. Instead of greedily accepting the opportunity to elevate himself, he vowed to do it only if God opened the door first. I've been convicted many times of wanting attention for myself. As a TV anchor, I've sought out celebrities as potential interview guests, obsessively refreshed my YouTube account to check for new subscribers, and became jealous and offended when others received big breaks instead of me. This behavior made me feel awful, and through repentance and a willing heart, I've been able to diminish the need for outside approval. Seek to bring glory to God only.

Surrender

Today I will pray for God to be glorified in everything I do.

God Honoring

If my people who are called by my name humble themselves, and pray and seek my face and turn from their wicked ways, then I will hear from heaven and will forgive their sin and heal their land.

2 CHRONICLES 7:14 ESV

We fickle humans search the world for solutions. We look to experts, doctors, and the people who seem to have all the answers. Having modern medicine and highly skilled workers is a blessing. But in our quest for help and healing, we must never put man before God. Throughout Scripture, we encounter frequent pleas from God to humble ourselves, to repent, and to seek his face. It's a pretty simple prescription—humility, sincere regret for how we've lived, and obedience—yet we often forsake it to spend our resources of time and money on fixes that ultimately fail. Unless we commit to biblical commands, any earthly solution is tenuous at best. If you've struggled in this area, take comfort in God's mercy and desire to rescue his people through simple repentance.

Surrender

Today I will seek God first and ask him to guide and direct my choices.

Better Together

"Where two or three are gathered in my name,
there am I among them."

MATTHEW 18:20 ESV

Substance abuse usually starts out as fun times with friends. But when partying progresses to addiction, the tables turn, and an activity that once promised relaxation and camaraderie turns to isolation and pain. Addiction is a progressive condition, and as time passes, tolerance for substances and sin increases along with shame and separation from God. Making the decision to repent from idolatry and turn to Jesus so he can restore our sanity is the first order of business. We cannot walk the recovery road alone, however. We need strong Christian discipleship and the support of others to remain on the straight path. There is strength in numbers, and when we come together in Jesus' name, he hears us and responds.

Surrender

Today I will pray for God to bring strong Christians to support and nurture my faith.

Straight from the Heart

Every way of a man is right in his own eyes,
but the LORD weighs the heart.

PROVERBS 21:2 ESV

Addicts can be extremely conniving creatures. Bondage to drugs and compulsive behaviors breeds manipulation and deception, and morals and values crumble like a stale cupcake. Though we might successfully trick others, trying to fool God is fruitless. He made us and perceives our innermost being, desires, and motives. He knows every thought we entertain and action we take. Why not get into alignment with him today? A new life in recovery means a restored heart and fresh purpose to live for God and die to the approval of man. Shedding the desire to please people brings exhilarating freedom. Sometimes doing things for the right reasons is hard, and we will battle our fleshly desires. But as we grow with Christ, he will slowly mold the wants of our hearts to his own.

Surrender

Today I pray God will help me have the right motives with everything I say and do.

Ripple Effect

"I will add fifteen years to your life. I will deliver you and this city out of the hand of the king of Assyria, and I will defend this city for my own sake and for my servant David's sake."

2 KINGS 20:6 ESV

A few years ago, I learned about a woman dying of cancer. I didn't know her well but strongly felt the Holy Spirit impressing on me the need to intercede. Her family was gathered around her hospital bed crying when I arrived, and they must've thought I was crazy. Still, they agreed to allowing me to pray over her. Through I fervently petitioned the Lord, she died the next day. Does this mean I should give up praying for others? Of course not! Sometimes healing doesn't happen, but we will never know unless we try. When we're willing vessels for God, anything is possible. I have never regretted praying for someone, and even in the situations where the outcome was not as I'd hoped, there is always an unseen ripple effect. God promises that his word will not return void. Our obedience will impact the people and the world around us.

Surrender

Today I will ask God for opportunities to pray for others and will be obedient about going where he leads me.

Be Willing

"'Behold, I stand at the door and knock. If anyone hears my voice and opens the door, I will come in to him and eat with him, and he with me.'"

REVELATION 3:20 ESV

Perhaps you've been seeking God for healing, restoration, or freedom from bondage. The first question you should ponder is: *Am I willing to stop doing the things that bring me sickness and pain?* My father passed away after refusing to give up alcohol, though many people offered their helping hands over the years. Failure to submit my will kept me in prison, too, but thank God my pain eventually crushed me to the point of surrender. Willingness holds the power to transform your life. You don't need to have the entire plan figured out. Just open the door a little crack and be receptive to change. Full surrender will transform your life. Jesus is waiting to take your hand and lead you into a bright, new future.

Surrender

Today I will ask God to help me become willing to change the habits and behaviors that are harming my relationship with him.

December

Fresh Fruit

Let all bitterness and wrath and anger and clamor and slander be put away from you, along with all malice.

EPHESIANS 4:31 ESV

Living in addiction brings a plethora of unwanted consequences. The slow form of suicide destroying our lives also invites a chaotic mix of behaviors that result from placing a drug or behavior before God. When we put down the bottle or the pipe, it's also time to do away with the sinful companions of resentment, anger, and strife and to allow the fruit of the Holy Spirit to replace them. As Jesus heals our hearts, we will become willing to sacrifice for others even when they don't deserve it. We begin to see every human through his eyes. Behaving in loving ways, even when we don't want to, will slowly change us. Our old sinful nature won't disappear overnight, but the pursuit of Jesus will always bring transformation in the end.

Surrender

Today I will ask God to help me overcome old sinful behaviors and to be filled with the fruit of the Spirit.

Joyful Giving

*Each one must give as he has decided in his heart,
not reluctantly or under compulsion,
for God loves a cheerful giver.*

2 CORINTHIANS 9:7 ESV

Giving can look different for everyone. For some, giving their time and effort in service is more doable than a financial contribution. My dad loved to tell my brother and me that "the Lord loves a cheerful giver" whenever he was delegating weekend chores to the two of us. Donating my weekend to housework caused much grumbling, and into adulthood, I ignored the biblical command to give. Belonging to a body of believers can sometimes feel like joining a big, dysfunctional family, with abundant opportunities to feel overworked, slighted, or offended. But despite messages about the importance of giving and the pressure to do your duty in the church nursery, tithing and serving should come from a willing heart. Ask Jesus for guidance about your specific situation.

Surrender

Today I pray for guidance with giving and serving and that I
will be obedient to God in these areas.

Truth Wins

Do your best to present yourself to God as one approved,
a worker who has no need to be ashamed,
rightly handling the word of truth.

2 TIMOTHY 2:15 ESV

Truth is becoming a precious commodity these days, with many too afraid to speak it for fear of offending someone. People are being cancelled for their obedient reverence to the Bible and for placing reality before subjective experiences or feelings. It's easy to get into heated conversations over cultural issues, and people are more divided than ever. Instead of trying to prove a point from your own experience, highlight the Word of God. In doing this, objections will come face-to-face with the Bible rather than trying to use human ability to win a debate. Prioritize proper handling of the Scriptures and an ability to articulate God's truth, and you'll always come out on top.

Surrender

Today I will pray for boldness and the ability to speak the truth in love.

Be the Church

"Go therefore and make disciples of all nations, baptizing them in the name of the Father and of the Son and of the Holy Spirit."

MATTHEW 28:19 ESV

Years ago, I visited a local church and heard the strangest sermon. The morning started out normally: coffee in the commons area, greetings from friendly people, and a fiery time of worship by a gifted team. But then things got a little odd. The pastor came out to deliver the message, took the mic, and yelled, "Go!" then left the stage while my husband and I exchanged perplexed looks. More context came the following week, with leadership emphasizing the need to take the message of Jesus to the streets and to fulfill the Great Commission. The purpose of church isn't just to chat with friends, sing songs, and drink coffee. It's bringing the gospel of Jesus Christ to a hurting world. May we remember the Lord's important final words before leaving earth.

Surrender

Today I will remember that I can be the church to everyone I meet.

Ask and Obey

"Get up, for it is your duty to tell us how to proceed in setting things straight. We are behind you, so be strong and take action."

EZRA 10:4 NLT

Sometimes we become so overwhelmed by our "to do" list that it becomes a "do nothing" list. During your prayer time today, ask God what action he wants you to take. Maybe he'll reveal a person to call, someone to pray for, or a project that needs attention. After you sense God's directives, write them down and follow through right away. If you're a procrastinator, be aware that the devil loves creating distractions and will do anything he can to keep you away from God's work. Make the Enemy mad by obeying right away, and don't make your heavenly Father ask you twice. When he sees that he can trust you in small matters, he will begin providing bigger opportunities to serve with greater blessings attached.

Surrender

Today I will spend time in prayer asking God what he wants me to accomplish today.

Choose to Submit

"If you turn away and refuse to listen, you will be devoured by the sword of your enemies. I, the LORD, have spoken!"

ISAIAH 1:20 NLT

Many teens and young people go through a time of rebellion. For some, the reasons are obvious: broken homes, dysfunctional parents, corrupt peer groups. Others may have had squeaky-clean upbringings, complete with stay-at-home moms and Girl Scout memberships, yet they still tumbled into addiction or New Age teachings. In either case, refusing to comply with God's commands will always bring increasing pain and turmoil. While I struggled to submit, God continued to urge, *We can do this the easy way or the hard way. It's your choice.* Refusing to listen to him carries serious consequences. Pursuing a life of sin can lead us to an early death and remove us from God's presence forever. Let today be the day you give everything to God.

Surrender

Today I pray for God to bring me into right standing with him.

You vs. You

This is the same mighty power that raised Christ from the dead and seated him in the place of honor at God's right hand in the heavenly realms.

EPHESIANS 1:19–20 NLT

It's easy to fall into the comparison game, becoming distracted by what others bring to the table and stacking their gifts and talents against yours. Making evaluations of people will ensure you're slipping outside God's will. Evaluating someone else will cause you to feel inferior or superior, and either scenario is displeasing to God. He has prepared good works for you that will pass by if you're coveting someone else's gifting. Commit today to compete only with yourself. When you catch yourself making comparisons, quickly repent and ask God to reveal the special purposes he has reserved just for you, and then share them with the world.

Surrender

Today I will ask God to show me what good works I can do today to further his kingdom.

Patience Is a Virtue

For everything there is a season,
a time for every activity under heaven.

ECCLESIASTES 3:1 NLT

In our microwave society, who doesn't struggle with patience? Who wants to wait? I often joke with my kids about childhood in the 1980s, when reaching someone by phone was only possible if they were at home because cell phones did not exist. We mailed letters, had pen pals, rode our bikes five miles to get an ice cream bar, and had to wait all week for a favorite television show to air. In our haste and rush, we must remember that God's timing is always perfect. If he requires us to wait, he surely has a reason and will teach us something if we are willing. Sometimes God has to get others ready before his plans for us can be fulfilled. Rest in knowing he is in control and working behind the scenes.

Surrender

Today I pray for patience and for God to teach me while I wait.

Love Actually

Dear children, let's not merely say that we love each other;
let us show the truth by our actions.

1 JOHN 3:18 NLT

Do you know someone who is all talk? Who makes grand plans that are never carried out, promises to pray from a distance but doesn't make an effort, or who claims to be a Christian yet walks right by a needy person? Talk is cheap, but acts of love will really get someone's attention. Consider the difference between casually telling your spouse to "have a good day" and mailing a love letter to their office or physically showing up at noon to take them out for lunch. Or instead of shaking someone's hand at church and then moving on, going below the superficial to search out hidden prayer needs. Go the extra mile to show people genuine care and not just fluffy talk. Let love be the reason that convinces others you are a true Christian.

Surrender

Today I will pray for a loving heart that truly seeks to bless others.

Deliver with Love

Love is patient and kind.
Love is not jealous or boastful or proud.

1 CORINTHIANS 13:4 NLT

Back when I was a teenager, I wanted to be popular, liked, and pretty. Nowadays, I value intelligence and humility much more than looking good. In my quest to grow in Bible knowledge, I come across many skilled and gifted teachers. Most are Christlike and seeking to bless others through their intelligence for the glory of God. But a few deliver all the smart goodies with an air of superiority but very little love. Everyone struggles with rudeness at times, but when boasting and condescension are constant companions, there is a problem. Let us seek to share with love what we have learned for the benefit of the kingdom and budding believers. May we never let biblical knowledge surpass our genuine love for others.

Surrender

Today I pray God will show me if I am approaching others with the wrong attitude.

Package Deal

> Peter replied, "Each of you must repent of your sins and turn to God, and be baptized in the name of Jesus Christ for the forgiveness of your sins. Then you will receive the gift of the Holy Spirit."
>
> ACTS 2:38 NLT

I've gone to extremes not only as an addict but also in church. After a straitlaced childhood spent in a reformed Presbyterian church, with my first round of sobriety I was thrust into a nondenominational church. My husband and I married as Lutherans and years later gravitated to an Assembly of God congregation, eventually landing somewhere in the middle of the two theologies. I've learned something from every pastor and house of worship I have passed through. Some barely mentioned the Holy Spirit, and others pushed him like a drug I didn't know I needed. Scripture teaches that we receive the Spirit when we accept Jesus and that greater filling can come at times. We should always seek the presence of God in greater measure while not forsaking the other important commandments in Scripture.

Surrender

Today I will ask Jesus for a greater filling of the Holy Spirit.

Surrender and Start

What good is it, dear brothers and sisters,
if you say you have faith but don't show it by your actions?
Can that kind of faith save anyone?

JAMES 2:14 NLT

Having faith in Jesus Christ is the cornerstone of our Christian beliefs. It is precisely how we know he was born of the Virgin Mary, died on the cross, and was resurrected on the third day. Faith enables us to believe without seeing, but it is not the whole story. We must put action behind it. As an addict, I was paralyzed with indecision and inertia—never able to finish anything. My penchant for procrastination kept goals and meaningful progress elusive. With addiction, we're forever spinning our wheels, trapped in a cycle of fakery and illusion of momentum. But a new start in Jesus enabled me to put my money where my mouth was. Wherever you are right now, stop and surrender. Pray for God to show you the next right step, and then do it. He will faithfully lead you from there.

Surrender

Today I will pray for God to show me what action to take,
and I will follow through.

Do It Scared

Because the Sovereign LORD helps me, I will not be disgraced.
Therefore, I have set my face like a stone, determined to do
his will. And I know that I will not be put to shame.

ISAIAH 50:7 NLT

You will never regret taking a stand for Jesus. A new drug-free life requires some acclimation time, and others close to you may not believe your conversion is genuine right away. Trust will rebuild over time with consistency and as true changes begin. Many who have overcome addictions are reformed people-pleasers or conflict avoiders like me, and at first, taking a stand can feel uncomfortable and threatening. Remember that Jesus promises to walk through every scary situation right beside you, and he offers a reward for honoring him before others. Make a commitment to never shrink back from an opportunity to bring glory to God.

Surrender

Today I pray for courage to be obedient to whatever God is calling me to do or say.

Wishful Thinking

We do this by keeping our eyes on Jesus, the champion who initiates and perfects our faith. Because of the joy awaiting him, he endured the cross, disregarding its shame. Now he is seated in the place of honor beside God's throne.

HEBREWS 12:2 NLT

If you wanted to, you would," is my pastor's sometimes aggravating but also entirely appropriate response to people "wishing" to do something. *Wish I could help. Wish I could attend. Wish I could tithe.* I've rolled my eyes in response to his comment at times, but honestly, the man of God is right. Every moment, we are always deciding what our focus will be, what action to take, and what we decide to prioritize and consider important. We will make time for those we love as well as activities that are important to us. Never forget that what you care about, pay attention to, talk about, and put energy behind is a *choice.* Make God the center of every day and allow him to set your first schedule and align your priorities with his.

Surrender

Today I will seek God right away and ask him to set my schedule.

Calling Heaven

To all who mourn in Israel, he will give a crown of beauty for ashes, a joyous blessing instead of mourning, festive praise instead of despair. In their righteousness, they will be like great oaks that the LORD has planted for his own glory.

ISAIAH 61:3 NLT

I've gone through periods of time—even in sobriety— where I just couldn't seem to shake the heaviness. I'd wake up weary, feel gloomy, and board the struggle bus. Unable to put my finger on what was wrong, I finally realized that adopting a garment of praise is always the solution. My gloom-solution-praise-routine starts with singing to the Lord. Anything really! "What a Friend We Have in Jesus" always works, and after belting out a song lifts my mood, I shift to gratitude and begin running through everything God has done. Reflecting upon his countless promises is miraculous, and then I repent for any leftover sins from the day before and start again. The Bible says the Lord inhabits the praises of his people. You simply cannot stay depressed when deliberately praising God. Call heaven down to elevate your mood through worship.

Surrender

Today I will sing praises to the Lord and thank him no matter how I feel.

Make It Count

Lazy people are soon poor;
hard workers get rich.

PROVERBS 10:4 NLT

While in the grips of addiction, I had a lot of trouble being productive. My first order of business after redemption came was to seek the Lord about my chaotic life. Now, each day starts in my prayer closet where I talk to God, read the Bible, and allow him to issue my marching orders for the day. *What are we doing today, Dad?* My list often includes praying for a friend, completing specific work-related tasks, or helping a child with homework. I also make sure to include some down time to read a book, serve someone, play with my dog, watch a (God-honoring) TV show or teaching, and exercise. Too much free time can turn into overthinking or temptation. Use your time wisely, strategize, and don't allow laziness to dull your focus.

Surrender

Today I will pray for help with prioritizing my day and using
time wisely.

Just Get Along

Live in harmony with each other. Don't be too proud to
enjoy the company of ordinary people.
And don't think you know it all!

ROMANS 12:16 NLT

We all know someone who insists on being right all
the time, and they usually are no picnic to be around.
Unfortunately, many Christians divide over issues that are
not vital to salvation. Some things are non-negotiable: the
Resurrection, the virgin birth, the deity of Jesus, the Trinity.
Others, we can just agree to disagree. Instead of trying to
prove accuracy in every situation, keep an open mind and be
willing to learn. No one has all the correct answers. Since I
came to faith in Jesus, my views have changed and evolved,
and I've rejected some beliefs as my walk has deepened. We
are all on a spiritual journey, so instead of tearing each other
down, let's do our best to live in harmony.

Surrender

Today I pray for an open mind and that I will not harm
another person's walk with Jesus.

Rock of Ages

This hope is a strong and trustworthy anchor for our souls.
It leads us through the curtain into God's inner sanctuary.

HEBREWS 6:19 NLT

A favorite childhood memory was going to a waterfront restaurant with my family called the Anchor Inn. I had never experienced an all-you-can-eat buffet before and was in heaven while overdosing on deep fried shrimp and frog legs. Sadly, that awesome joint eventually closed down and became some other establishment. Jesus, however, is the anchor of our souls who will never leave, run short on love, or fail. Sometimes it might be hard to discern what he is up to, especially when waiting patiently for something or not sensing his presence. Being his disciple requires a choice: Will we anchor ourselves to an ever-changing culture or in the rock of ages? Depending on the world is risky business destined for failure.

Surrender

Today I will pray for peace in knowing that Jesus anchors
my soul with his enduring love.

Holy Distributors

On the last day, the climax of the festival,
Jesus stood and shouted to the crowds,
"Anyone who is thirsty may come to me!"

JOHN 7:37 NLT

I've sampled a few home sales businesses in an effort to make a fast buck. Amway, Beachbody, Pampered Chef, Creative Memories. I gave lingerie parties a shot, which became drunken bashes rivaling my frat house days. Along the way, I met some folks who hustled and did quite well with these entrepreneurial opportunities. A little grit is all it takes. My pastor has a different take on distribution. His favorite catch phrase from the pulpit involves spreading the contagious power of the gospel in the following format: receive, contain, and broadcast. Receive power and guidance through prayer, contain it within your heart, and then broadcast it to the world. That's a sales pitch we should all embrace.

Surrender

Today I will receive power from the Holy Spirit through prayer and share it with others.

Spiritual Fight

"Look, I have given you authority over all the power of the enemy, and you can walk among snakes and scorpions and crush them. Nothing will injure you."

LUKE 10:19 NLT

My good friend is a deliverance minister. His take on the demonic realm is simple, "When in doubt, cast it out." Did you know that as a spirit-filled believer, you have the authority to rebuke demons? There isn't a devil under every pillow, and I don't believe Christians can be possessed by them, but the spirit realm is very real. Even after accepting Jesus, we can be oppressed or afflicted by demons. Don't let this disturb you. Just remember that Jesus Christ offers his name to cast out the demonic forces. Don't spend another day feeling harassed, tormented, or bothered. Do away with the demons yourself or enlist the help of a church team who specializes in deliverance.

Surrender

Today I will take up my authority in Jesus by rebuking the devil and his demons.

Believe in the Impossible

He touched their eyes and said,
"Because of your faith, it will happen."
MATTHEW 9:29 NLT

The debate over whether the gifts of the Holy Spirit are still actively moving today rages on. Were the miraculous signs, healings, and wonders we read about in the book of Acts and other parts of the New Testament just for the early church? Or do they still transform lives today? Every week, I see the Holy Spirit dramatically change people through my work, yet I still remain cautious about more dramatic reports: paralytics walking, dead people rising, and grave illnesses entering remission. Just because I haven't seen it doesn't mean God isn't on the move. While we should always pray for God's will to be done, the Bible clearly shows that *belief* and *faith* are two very important factors involved with answered prayer.

Surrender

Today I will ask for God to increase my faith and belief that he will move on my behalf.

People Are People

Don't boast about following a particular human leader.
For everything belongs to you.

1 CORINTHIANS 3:21 NLT

I've gotten starry-eyed over famous folks more times than I care to admit. Politicians, rock stars, influencers, and newscasters have cast a spell with their superior skills and compelling charisma. Putting someone on a pedestal and rabidly following every move on social or broadcast media can bring disappointment when these folks show their flaws or fall from grace. After going "all in" for influencers and being convicted of idolatry, I brought this problem to the Lord. He revealed my unhealed areas, and I stopped trying to make connections with the famous. God can still open doors on my behalf, but I've surrendered kicking them open. If you can relate, ask God to expose root causes, and pray for help with overcoming idolatry.

Surrender

Today I pray that I will be no respecter of persons and will see others as people with different opportunities.

Kingdom Love

"Do to others as you would like them to do to you."
LUKE 6:31 NLT

The intoxication of a new love always left me spellbound. Combined with excessive binge drinking, the short-term results of casual flings were absolutely mind blowing. From age fourteen, I pursued the opposite sex as a medication for inner turmoil. Approaching a new courtship felt very much like heading out on a Friday night: preparation, anticipation, dopamine—then drunkenness, blackout, and shame. The "love" I pursued revealed itself to be lust and a deep need for acceptance with no solid or lasting foundation. If you've been pursuing relationships outside God's will, instead commit to Jesus. A marriage built on love, not lust, is the goal. Ask the Lord to send that special person and trust his timing. And if you're happy being single, great! You'll be able to serve the Lord more completely.

Surrender

Today I will pray for God to help me wait for my kingdom spouse and for help to serve him more completely.

Stop Selling

People who aren't spiritual can't receive these truths from God's Spirit. It all sounds foolish to them and they can't understand it, for only those who are spiritual can understand what the Spirit means.

1 CORINTHIANS 2:14 NLT

Have you ever felt like you're talking to a brick wall? After God changes us through no power of our own, we naturally want to shout it from the mountaintops. We should desire that everyone experience the freedom and joy that comes from surrendering to Jesus. Yet others may meet with apathy and glassy eyes our newfound zeal to witness. The gospel is not a sales pitch. Simply share your testimony and pray for the Holy Spirit to step in and influence whomever you're speaking to. He will faithfully show you what say. It's not our job to convince anyone through manipulation tactics or charming talk. God alone has the power to change hearts. We are simply his vessel, and we should always remember the power in living as solid witnesses for Christ.

Surrender

Today I pray for willingness to share my testimony and for God to use my words to help others.

Faithful Living

Commit everything you do to the LORD. Trust him, and
he will help you. He will make your innocence radiate like
the dawn, and the justice of your cause will shine like the
noonday sun.

PSALM 37:5–6 NLT

Some people fear the potential consequences of going "all
in." They favor cohabitation over marriage, avoid making
promises, and sidestep other Christians who will hold them
accountable. Wavering between my desire to drink and my
need to stop led to ongoing failures until I got miserable
enough to abandon drinking for good. Commitment is a
big deal; it means you are completely dedicated to someone
or something. Scripture says when you submit to the Lord,
he will act. After I made the decision to dedicate myself to
serving him, a life that had seemed like stalled machinery
began to move forward. Putting God first through complete
trust lifts the heavy load of fear that comes from trying to
control and manipulate people and situations. Allow Jesus to
lead the way, and he will faithfully illuminate your path.

Surrender

Today I will commit to putting God first and allowing him
to lead my life.

Hold Steady

Let's not get tired of doing what is good. At just the right time we will reap a harvest of blessing if we don't give up.

GALATIANS 6:9 NLT

Wanting instant change in exchange for good behavior is a normal human response. After overcoming addiction, it's natural to think everything else in life will also fall into place. Breaking free from addictive vices is essential to allowing God to use you as his vessel, but there's still a long road ahead. Some days you'll feel on top of the world, making great strides toward your goals, and at other times, you'll barely hold on to keep from falling into a ditch. Giving in to temptation only helps temporarily and makes things so much worse in the long run. Take heart in knowing God is refining you in both good times and bad. Doing the next right thing and focusing on submitting to his will each day will eventually yield a storehouse of treasures for the kingdom. It is okay to hold steady.

Surrender

Today I will take a deep breath and remember to trust God and just do the next right thing.

Open Your Heart

> He heals the brokenhearted
> and bandages their wounds.
>
> PSALM 147:3 NLT

Some wounds run very deep. Many who battle addictions are trying desperately to use drugs and alcohol to mask pain from abandonment, trauma, anxiety, and other stressors. When my husband and I experienced brokenness in our marriage, my knee-jerk reaction was to do everything I could to fix us. At my wits' end, I cried out to a friend, who suggested I let Jesus heal my heart. The concept felt so foreign at the time that I didn't even know where to begin. The good news was that I didn't need to figure everything out; once I surrendered the problem to him, Jesus faithfully led me to the right people and places. I began meditating on the promises in Scripture, and when I opened my bruised heart through prayer and quiet time, I was flooded with his peace. Bring your hopelessness and broken pieces to Jesus, you'll be amazed at what he will do.

Surrender

Today I will ask Jesus to flood my broken places with his love.

Finding Freedom

Be kind and compassionate to one another,
forgiving each other, just as in Christ God forgave you.

EPHESIANS 4:32 NIV

Unforgiveness will trap us in the worst type of bondage in which we grant the devil and his demons access to our lives. Harboring resentment and offense toward those who have done us harm serves no real purpose and keeps us in chains, unable to break free. The Bible commands that we not only forgive our enemies but also pray for them. The highest level of this act of grace is actually asking God to *bless* your worst adversaries. If that feels like a tall order right now, don't despair—it may take years to fully get there. That's okay; willingness is all you need. Decide to forgive whether you feel like it or not. How others respond doesn't matter. Forgiveness sets you free and enables you to move to new levels with Jesus.

Surrender

Today I will pray for willingness to forgive people who have harmed me.

Speak Up

Speak up for those who cannot speak for themselves,
for the rights of all who are destitute.

PROVERBS 31:8 NIV

I heard a quote that really stuck with me. In a famous public address, Reverend Martin Luther King Jr. said, "A man dies when he refuses to stand up for that which is right. A man dies when he refuses to stand up for justice. A man dies when he refuses to take a stand for that which is true."[5] As an addict, I didn't care about much except covering up my lies. When someone asked for my opinion on something, even as simple as my favorite restaurant, I found it extremely difficult to articulate myself, much less clarify my stance on controversial issues. These days, I am serious about what matters to God, and I refuse to remain complicit in someone else's sin or God-dishonoring practice. As you grow in recovery, God will reveal when he wants you to speak up. Work hard to become biblically literate so that you can defend the truth of Jesus Christ.

Surrender

Today I will pray for boldness in speaking up about issues
that matter to God.

---

5   Frederick W. Mayer, *Narrative Politics: Stories and Collective Action*
    (Oxford, UK: Oxford University Press, 2014), 133.

Boundaries

"I am the gate; whoever enters through me will be saved.
They will come in and go out, and find pasture."

JOHN 10:9 NIV

Addicts have notoriously poor boundaries. We
compromise ourselves and our values for the sake of
approval, drinking buddies, and a brief hit of self-worth. The
company we keep often invites opportunities for others to
use us, abuse us, and push us to accept their poor treatment.
But when we submit to Jesus and are restored through belief
in him and repentance of sin, we are transformed. We begin
to see ourselves as God does: beautiful, cherished, and
unique. We realize that whenever we were treated poorly by
others, it was because we allowed it. With the Lord's help,
we begin to love, nurture, and care not only for ourselves
but also for others. We learn to enforce boundaries, which
communicate to the world that we will no longer tolerate
abuse because we deserve to be valued. Our heavenly Father
says so.

Surrender

Today I will see myself as God does, cherished, valued,
and unique.

Your Time

"If you remain silent at this time, relief and deliverance for the Jews will arise from another place, but you and your father's family will perish. And who knows but that you have come to your royal position for such a time as this?"

ESTHER 4:14 NIV

Sometimes it feels like we're all alone in the world. We constantly struggle just to be noticed and feel forced to fight, claw, and wrestle our way to the top. For example, when I was offered the position of executive director at the Lindell Recovery Network, I thought it was a mistake and would soon be withdrawn. Certainly, someone more qualified, skilled, articulate, and captivating should have the position. But that was God's plan for me. He makes plans for each of us that only *we* can fulfill. There's no need to jockey for position, compete, or worry that the Lord will give away his plan for you to someone else. He designed you for a unique kingdom role. Relax, believe it, and simply do the next right thing. If you're willing to repent and fully submit to him, God will elevate you beyond your wildest dreams.

Surrender

Today I pray God will help me fulfill his divine plan for my life.